30-

THE PEE WEE REESE STORY

BOOKS BY GENE SCHOOR

CASEY STENGEL: *Baseball's Greatest Manager*

CHRISTY MATHEWSON: *Baseball's Greatest Pitcher*

THE JACK DEMPSEY STORY

THE JIM THORPE STORY: *America's Greatest Athlete*

THE LEO DUROCHER STORY

THE PEE WEE REESE STORY

RED GRANGE: *Football's Greatest Halfback*

THE STAN MUSIAL STORY

THE STORY OF TY COBB: *Baseball's Greatest Player*

THE TED WILLIAMS STORY

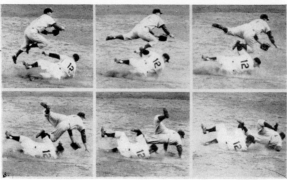

Reese flies through the air after getting ball off to first to complete eighth-inning double play in 1955 World Series.

Reese receives the Sid Mercer Memorial Award as "Player of the Year." Geo. M. Weiss, vice president and general manager of the New York Yankees, receives the Bill Slocum Meritorious Service Award.

Pee Wee with his wife, daughter and mother in the car he got on Pee Wee Reese Night at Ebbets Field.

Reese, one time marble champ swaps his cap for the crown of the 1951 marble champ.

A favorite of the small fry, Pee Wee is surrounded by fans in Vero Beach.

1941—Reese gets some pointers from Max Carey.

1955—Manager Walter Alston and the Dodgers ju
before the World Series.

1946—Leading Brooklyn hitters—Reiser, Stanky,
Walker and Reese.

1955—At spring training—Fernandez, Zimmer,
Reese, Gilliam and Neal.

1948—Reese, Durocher and Branca of the Brooklyn Dodgers.

Pee Wee Reese and Jackie Robinson limber up at
spring training.

THE
PEE WEE
REESE
STORY

BY GENE SCHOOR

JULIAN MESSNER, INC.

NEW YORK

Published by Julian Messner, Inc.
8 West 40th Street, New York 18

Published simultaneously in Canada
by The Copp Clark Company, Ltd.

Library of Congress Catalog Card No. 56-6795

Third Printing, 1957

MANUFACTURED IN THE UNITED STATES OF AMERICA
BY GEORGE MC KIBBIN & SON; BROOKLYN, NEW YORK

Photographs used with the permission of Wide World Photos

To Barry Butner

A Pee Wee Reese fan for all of his young life

In grateful acknowledgment to MILT SHAPIRO *for his help in the preparation of this book*

CHAPTER 1

Pitcher Jake Mooty turned his back on home plate and looked at the scoreboard, deep in center field. He squinted in the hot June sun, wiped the perspiration from his tanned face.

"I've got to work on this next hitter. He's the new shortstop for the Dodgers. Everybody—all the scouts are talking about him. He's fast, small, strong and wiry, sprays hits to all fields. Good line drive hitter, no known weakness." He chuckled to himself as he faced the Dodger shortfielder.

"No weakness," he spit. "Well, I'll show this busher a thing or two. Score is tied 3–3. If I get this kid, we can pick up a run in the thirteenth inning—maybe pull the game right out of the fire."

Mooty nodded to his catcher, hitched his pants and toed the rubber for the big pitch. The Brooklyn batter cocked his bat as Mooty went into his windup. It was a fast-breaking curve that just nicked the outside corner of the plate. The Dodger rookie shook his head. "Lucky," he muttered. "Throw me another one like that and I'll show you! Hit it a mile—yeah—win the game right now!"

Mooty snarled at the busher, toed the rubber again. The pitch had to be good, but not too good. The batter waved his big stick menacingly.

"C'mon let's have it."

Mooty took his full windup. He put everything on the ball. It was a blinding fast ball that was shoulder high—but no—he shouted across at the batter, "Look out, it slipped."

The words froze in his throat. Horror stricken, he watched as the ball sped toward the batter, who stood there, waiting, leaning into the plate as if he expected the speeding pitch to break into another curve.

But the pitch didn't break! Mooty stood paralyzed as the ball crashed with a heart-stopping "thwuck" against the side of the batter's head.

There was a frozen moment, then the young Brooklyn player pitched over on his face. He lay still across home plate as the ball bounced crazily along the first base line.

Then a great roar of anguish broke from the crowd, as both Dodger players and Chicago players dashed to the stricken ballplayer, who lay inert.

"Get out of the way. Give the kid some air," snarled manager Leo Durocher, elbowing his way to the fallen player's side. "Get the doctor—C'mon now, let's have some help—now. The kid's badly hurt. Doc—Doc Wendler!"

"Here, Leo. I'll take care of everything—Let's not wait. Get a stretcher here fast! I'm going to take the boy to the hospital. He's been hit bad. We've got to get him to the hospital right now."

Durocher nodded without looking up. He helped the attendants lift the unconscious player onto the stretcher. He patted the still form, peered into the boyish face and said in a voice choked with tears, "Doc, go with him. Get him the best of everything. I want to get him the very best treatment. Understand, Doc? And call me just as soon as the doctors look at him. Hear me, Doc?"

Wendler nodded. "Okay, Leo. Now easy with him, fellas. Lift him easy."

Leo stood aside as four ushers gently lifted the young Dodger shortstop and carried him to the waiting ambulance.

Two white-coated attendants silently lifted the stretcher into the ambulance. The doors closed and the car sped through the busy Chicago streets to the hospital.

At the hospital brain specialists busily probed the effects of the Dodger ballplayer's injury.

"I think he'll be all right, Leo." It was Doc Wendler on the phone to Durocher at the clubhouse. "He came to in the ambulance and asked about the ball game. The doctors say he'll have to be here at the hospital for at least forty-eight hours for observation."

After that day's game, the Dodger clubhouse was a subdued place. They had not only lost their bright young shortstop in a freak accident, but had lost the ball game, too, in the twelfth inning when Chicago's Al Todd belted a home run off pitcher Tot Presnell.

The beaning of their teammate had a sobering effect on the normally high-spirited Dodger crew. This youngster, in the major leagues just a few short weeks, had impressed them all with his sure fielding and quiet, gracious manner. This was only June 1st of the 1940 season, and the rookie shortstop was already a popular member of the veteran Dodger gang, without indulging in the boisterous, backslapping kind of friendliness they might have resented in a green busher. No, this kid was just a nice

· 11 ·

guy, and he looked great at the shortstop post, a position he had wrested from manager Durocher.

Not the least of those impressed by the young infielder was manager Durocher. To the surprise of the fans, the Dodger players and Brooklyn president Larry McPhail, the volatile Dodger pilot seemed to be handing over his own cherished shortstop position to this rookie on a silver platter.

This wasn't like Durocher, who had fought tooth and nail every foot of his colorful way in baseball. Leo, letting this busher walk right in and take over his glove at shortstop? It didn't seem possible.

But Durocher, even in his spitfire days of 1940, was above all else an honest appraiser. He recognized his slowness of foot and his aching muscles for what they were—warnings that it was time for Leo to forget about shortstopping and play out his hand solely as a manager. And this kid was good, darned good. Durocher knew it from the first day he saw him. "Covers the left side of the infield like an octopus," he had remarked to a sports writer during spring training.

But now, in the clubhouse, Durocher thought grimly of the youngster lying in the hospital, and he shook his head.

"Doc," he said to Wendler, when the trainer returned from the hospital, "What do you think?"

"It's really difficult to say, Leo," Wendler shrugged. "The boy was hit solidly, there's no doubt about that. It's fifty-fifty I guess, whether it's a fracture or a concussion. All we can do is hope, until we get the report from the X rays tomorrow."

"I didn't mean that, Doc." Durocher said. "I mean

how do you think it'll affect the kid when he comes back? You think this'll ruin him for the game? Do you think he'll be any good to us any more."

"How so, Leo?" Wendler said.

"Well, I've been sitting here thinking," Durocher said slowly. "Thinking about all the guys I knew or had heard about who never were the same again after they got beaned. You must know a couple of cases, too, Doc. Some guys shrug it off and come back to beat everybody's brains out. But there are some that are always plate shy after they've been hurt like that. They back off from the inside pitches. They fall away from tight curves. They're finished as hitters. And before long, they're finished in baseball," Durocher sighed heavily. "I sure hope it doesn't happen to this kid, Doc," the manager added feelingly. "I sure hope not. But I just don't know."

And who could blame Durocher for doubting, hoping? For who, indeed, could have foretold that the young rookie lying in a hospital bed, his head swathed in bandages, would bounce back to play sensational baseball until a cruel Fate would step in and lay him low with a serious injury later again that season? Who would have dared predict that dismal afternoon of June 1, 1940, that Harold "Pee Wee" Reese would lead the Brooklyn Dodgers to the pennant that following season, then go on to become one of Brooklyn's most revered and respected players, and one of the greatest shortstops in the game?

CHAPTER **2**

The summer sun rose hot and bright, its rays glinting on hundreds of windows, waking the citizens of Ekron, Kentucky to the new day. On Elm Street a dog barked at a passing bakery wagon, the horse's hooves clip-clopping loudly on the cobblestones; from the distant railroad yards of neighboring Louisville, the chug of a locomotive engine could be heard, and if you'd been standing in the bell tower of the local firehouse you could have seen the puffs of white smoke. Down Grove Street came the Abner Brothers with their ice wagon, making their deliveries to the butcher and the vegetable man, the grocer and the ice cream parlor, same as they did every morning. The town was beginning to stir.

Old Mr. Ellison, as usual, was the first to open his store —Ellison's, Hardware and General Merchandise. He stepped inside and sniffed, as he always did, at the familiar, not unpleasant mixture of sawdust, feed and fertilizer. He looked up at the picture on the seed company calendar, then ripped off the top page. Today was the twenty-third of July, 1919. Mr. Ellison's head turned from the calendar at a noise from the street outside. "Sounds like a rig," he said to himself, half aloud. "Kinda early for a rig to be out riding." He stepped to the doorway and watched the carriage clatter swiftly down the street till it disappeared around a corner at full speed, teetering dangerously.

The storekeeper pursed his lips. "Now where could Doc be going—all fired up like that?" he mused. He mentally ticked off on his fingers all the known sick and the expectant mothers in Ekron.

The sun was nearing its zenith when the doctor's carriage passed Ellison's store again, the horse trotting at an easy gait. The storekeeper stepped into the street and called to the tired-looking figure holding the reins.

"What was it, Doc?" Ellison asked, for he had already learned, the way storekeepers inevitably do in a town like Ekron, that the doctor had been at Mrs. Reese's.

The physician turned in his seat. "Boy," he called to the storekeeper. Then he turned again and drove on.

Mr. Ellison walked back into his shop and nodded to himself, almost with satisfaction, it seemed, as if he were giving his grudging approval to the mother for having done what was right and proper by everyone. A growing town like Ekron needed boys.

In the Reese household the shades had been drawn against the noonday sun, and it was cool in the bedroom, next to the kitchen, where Mrs. Reese lay, pale and smiling, in the large iron bed.

"He isn't very big, is he, Carl?" she said, looking at the pink, wrinkled infant at her side.

"Big enough for a baby, I guess, Emma," her husband smiled. "Time enough for him to grow. Before you know it you'll be chasing him away from the icebox and shooing him outside to play." He bent and kissed his wife.

"You rest now, Emma. I'll fix us both something for lunch. I guess the chores can wait a little while."

Emma Reese lay back on the pillow and closed her eyes, exhausted, but she was content. Suddenly she opened her eyes.

"Carl," she called to her husband, busying himself in the kitchen.

"Yes, Emma?"

"What do you think he will be when he grows up?"

Carl Reese chuckled affectionately. "Well, if he turns out to be a dumb cluck like his old man, he'll probably wind up being a farmer."

"Now, Carl," his wife admonished. "You're a lot smarter than you like to give yourself credit for. There's men in these parts don't have brains enough to sign their name, much less do all the book reading you do."

"Well, you may be right on that account, Emma," her husband admitted, as he carried in a bowl of steaming broth and set it on a table at his wife's bedside. "Doc was telling me about some old buzzard of a farm hand he's been treating the past couple of months. Seems every time the doc makes out a prescription, this old buzzard looks at it and says, 'That's the stuff'll do it, Doc.' The old fool doesn't even know the thing ain't written in English!"

Emma Reese smiled. "The doc and his stories!" She looked down at her new son. "Maybe Harold here'll be a doctor someday."

"And get up in the middle of the night every time some old biddy's got a headache? And everybody in town owin' him money? He'd be a lot better off being a farmer. At least you don't have to listen to people's troubles all day long," he grinned. "You don't even have time enough to think of your own."

"Oh, Carl, you're always joking," his wife pouted good humoredly. "Let me have my soup."

Carl Reese sat silently thinking his thoughts as he watched his wife sip the hot soup. When she finished he removed the bowl and went into the kitchen, rinsed the dish and the spoon, dried them and put them away. When he came back into the bedroom his wife was fast asleep, her long brown hair spread against the white pillow.

He sat down on the straight-backed wooden chair beside her bed. And there he sat for many minutes, looking at his wife and son with loving and wondering eyes. Then, suddenly, a thought came to him, and he cocked his head as if listening to what his mind had to say.

"Well, why not a baseball player?" he said aloud, finally. "Look at fellas like Babe Ruth and Ty Cobb. They make a lot of money, and they're famous and respected and all. If things'd been different, and I was a little younger, I might of made the big leagues myself." He said it almost belligerently, talking now to the two slumbering figures in the bed. "I'm no small potatoes around the semipro leagues in Louisville, you know. I make more than five dollars a game, and I'm no big-leaguer. Guess I started to play baseball too late. But you, son, I'm gonna start teaching you how to play ball real early, and you're going to be a good player. Make your mom and me real proud of you."

Then he stood up and leaned over the bed, peering intently at his wrinkled-faced son, sleeping the untroubled sleep of the newborn. He sat down again and looked doubtfully at the infant. "It's true enough, though," Carl Reese said to Harold K. Reese, not quite four hours old. "You do look kinda small for your age."

CHAPTER 3

The youngsters stood in a ragged-looking cluster around the barrier of wood and chicken wire that served as a backstop behind home plate. "I'll take Hank," said one of the tallest of the group, indicating a dark-haired youngster in baggy knickerbockers. "I'll take Denny," said another of the taller, apparently older boys of the troupe. "I'll take Billy," came back the first boy. "Dick," countered the other. And as they continued choosing the two teams for their sandlot baseball game, on the fringe of the group an anxious-eyed kid, smaller than all the rest, jumped up and down eagerly.

"How about me, how about me?" he called, as the sides were picked and still his name was not mentioned. Finally, one of the team captains looked down at the pint-sized youngster. "Okay, Harold's the only guy left. I guess I got him."

As they trotted out to take their positions on the field, the sandy-haired youngster named Harold headed for the shortstop position.

"Hey, kid, where you think you're goin'?" called the tall boy who had resignedly chosen him to play.

"I want to play short," Harold Reese said, although he knew they would never let him play the infield. But he always hoped to bluff his way into his cherished position by boldly taking his place at the shortstop post.

"Hah!" the team captain scoffed. "Maybe you want to take my place on the pitcher's mound, too?" He pointed to the weed-covered expanse on the edge of the lot. "Out in left field, kid, where you always go. You ought to be glad we're even letting you play."

Reese scuffed at the dirt with his shoes, but he went out to left field. At least, he thought bitterly to himself, I'm playing. But someday, someday I'm going to get to play in that infield. Then I'll show those guys!

But "those guys" were in no hurry to be shown. And despite the fact that Harold Reese grew in skill, he didn't grow in size, and his playing was restricted to the outfield.

Not every afternoon, however. Several years earlier, the Reeses had given up their unprofitable struggle with the farm and moved to Louisville, where Carl Reese obtained a job as detective for the Louisville and Nashville Railroad. There were times when Harold's father worked the night shift at the railroad, and it was on these afternoons that the two Reeses built a foundation of quiet skill and poise in young Harold that was to enable him to stand up to the major leagues' roughest weather in a few short years.

The elder Reese dearly hoped that his promising son might go on to fulfill an ambition that he himself had only partially realized. And Harold just as sorely wanted to play baseball. Still in knee pants, not yet in high school, he had formed this ambition. And with it, the determination.

"Get down!" Carl Reese would shout to his son, as he batted grounders to him hour after hour. "You got to dig that ball out of the ground, boy! Stay with it! Play the ball. Don't let it play you!" They kept at it till the sinking sun forced them homeward. His arm around his boy's shoulder, his voice, unnaturally loud in the stillness of the twilight, Carl Reese explained what he could about how the infield should be played. He probed deeply into the memory of his experience, trying to come up with some incident, some fact, some piece of information that would add the slightest bit to Harold's knowledge and skill.

If Harold Reese's career in sandlot baseball was limited to shagging an occasional fly ball that ventured his weedy way in the outfield, his career in another field, at least, was more glorious.

Reese was a crackerjack marbles shooter, and he spared no effort in gaining revenge on his taunters on the baseball field by beating them regularly in marble games. "Oh, oh, here comes Harold," the players would grumble. "We're sunk now." And Reese, grinning, would put his hand in his marbles bag and draw out a small, crystal-clear specimen. "You guys don't stand a chance," he'd say. "I've got my favorite peewee with me today."

"Man, peewee ought to be your middle name, the way you use that shooter," one of the youngsters said admiringly one day.

So it became "Here comes Pee Wee," instead of Harold. And in 1932, when the sharpshooting marbles player went on to win the runner-up spot in the national marbles tournament, the nickname was cemented on.

He won another great victory that same year. "Hey, Pop," he yelled one spring afternoon, barging into the kitchen where his father was sitting down to lunch. "Guess what, Pop!"

Carl Reese looked up from the table. "Don't tell me," he said. "The Yankees have signed you to a contract."

"Aw, Pop," Pee Wee said, poutingly, "You're always kidding. But it's almost as good as that. Well, not really almost. But anyway, I'm going to play in the American Legion League this year. With the Eclipse Juniors. They asked me. I didn't even ask them!"

His father grinned approvingly. "Well, they play on a good field. At least you won't get poison ivy chasing fly balls through the weeds any more."

"But that's the best part of all, Pop," Pee Wee said excitingly. "I'm not playing the outfield. I'm going to play second base!"

"What's all the excitement?" Pee Wee's mother broke in, bustling into the kitchen. "Harold, leave your father alone. He has to get to work early today. When you two get together talking about baseball you're harder to stop than a couple of back yard gossips."

"Now, now, Emma," Carl Reese grinned. "No scolding. Guess what happened to our boy today."

"I know," she said. "He stole a base hit, or he threw a home run, or something, and he won the game in the ninth round. Or maybe he brought home a nice note from his teacher—for once."

Carl Reese chuckled and looked at his son. "See, son," he said. "You can't win. Go in and do your homework now, and we'll talk about this tomorrow."

When Pee Wee had gone, Carl Reese turned to his wife. "Now, Emma," he said easily, "you shouldn't take the boy's baseball so lightly. It means a lot to him."

"I know, Carl," she returned gently. "And I don't mind his playing at all. But really, the way you two carry on sometimes you'd think that's all there was in the world."

"For Harold, that's all there is."

"That's just what I mean, Carl," Emma Reese said. "I'm not sure it's such a good idea, your encouraging him like this. It's all right to play baseball as a pastime or to make a little extra money on week ends, like you used to. But for a living! Who ever heard of such a thing?"

"Emma, you know better than that," returned her husband. "Why, in the major leagues a man makes a darned good living! Lots of ballplayers make more in a year than I make in ten years."

"So do bank presidents. And while you're dreaming, how about making yourself head of the railroad?"

"But Emma, that boy's got what it takes. I know it. For a kid his age he's good. He uses his head. He learns things. And what I wanted to tell you about today is that he's going to play second base for the Eclipse Juniors. They're a regular American Legion team. You've got to be a little better than average to play in that league."

"Oh, Carl," Emma Reese said tiredly. "I'm just trying to be realistic about this. Sometimes you talk like a small boy yourself. I don't mean to discourage you or Harold, there's a lifetime of difference between these Eclipses and professional baseball, now isn't there, Carl? Harold'll be going to high school soon. He should be thinking about a trade to study or about going to college. Baseball, that's just a dream for boys."

Carl Reese stared at the white tablecloth a long time before answering his wife. "Maybe you're right, Emma," he said at last. "But I remember what I once read in a book. 'Without the dream, there can never be the reality,' it said. He's got the dream, Emma. Maybe we ought to give him the chance to make it come true."

The dream was beginning to fade in Pee Wee Reese. Though he had caught on with the New Covenant Presbyterian Church team, an advance, in a way, from the American Legion League of the year before, he was shunted from position to position. And at fourteen, when he entered DuPont Manual Training High School, he weighed less than one hundred pounds. It appeared he'd always be too puny to make a real baseball player. Pee Wee was not very happy. He did stretching exercises to grow tall; ate five meals a day; played ball all afternoon. But nothing helped.

Still, in his junior year at Manual, Reese decided to make his bid for the school team. He had little hope of getting on, but he knew how proud it would make his father if he did. At least he could say he tried.

It was a fine spring day, with just a little late winter crispness left in the air to make it sharp and clean. His heart pounding in his chest, Reese walked stiffly out to the playing field to report for the first practice. The sharp crack of the bat came to his ears as he neared the field, and also the chatter of the players. He licked his lips nervously. He wanted to run away. Almost without realizing it, he hoped somebody would call him aside, prevent his trying out today, so that he wouldn't be embarrassed by what he felt would be his certain failure.

But he found himself walking toward the batting cage, where the DuPont coach stood talking with a cluster of uniformed players. As Reese approached, the other fellows looked bigger and bigger in his eyes. They seemed to be giants compared to his own undersized frame. He felt the boys staring at him, grinning at him, ready to burst out laughing at this skinny kid wanting to play baseball on the high school team.

Pee Wee got to within a few yards of the coach. He stopped. He couldn't go on. He turned quickly, his eyes blurring, and ran from the field, the tears running hotly down his cheeks.

"I couldn't do it, Pop," he cried to his father that evening. They were sitting in the living room, father and son, talking about the afternoon's incident. "I felt they'd all laugh at me if I told them I wanted to try out for the team. Those guys are ten times bigger than I am. I'll never be any good to play ball. I'm just too small."

"Don't let it get you down, son." Carl Reese was all sympathy. "Sure, we're disappointed you can't make the team. Even Mom and your sisters are rootin' for you. But you've got another year to go. Maybe you'll develop some muscle and can go at it again. Meanwhile, you just keep pluggin' away with the New Covenant team. That's just as good experience. Billy Herman of the Cubs played with them when he was a kid, you know."

"Yes, I know, Pop, but he wasn't small like I am," Pee Wee said discouragingly.

But Reese kept plugging away at the game, playing his heart out with the New Covenant team, and getting into pickup games at the local parks whenever he could. It was in these park games, sparkling at second base, that Pee Wee's future began to take shape.

He would hop around the keystone sack like a jack rabbit, grabbing every ball within reach, diving headlong for those beyond it. After one such game, in which Pee Wee had starred by driving home the winning runs with a double and making several spectacular plays at second, he was approached by the young instructor at the park.

"You play a pretty fine second base, there, young fella," Roy Bali said to Reese.

"Thanks," returned Pee Wee, grinning through his sweat-streaked face. "I try my best."

"You go to school around here?" asked Bali.

Pee Wee nodded. "DuPont High."

"You play on the team?"

"No."

"How come? You're pretty good."

Reese was beginning to feel uneasy. "I don't know," he fidgeted. "I don't have the time. I got to study and everything. I just didn't think about it, I guess. And I'm not too big," he added ruefully.

Bali looked keenly at the youngster's troubled face. He took in the short stature, the slight build. And he understood. "Well," he said to Pee Wee, "just keep coming around here and playing. Maybe you and I can get together and teach each other a few things. I play a little ball myself."

Reese was anxious to break away from the instructor and his uncomfortable questions. "Yeah. Well, I'll see you around," he said hurriedly, and raced from the park.

Bali stood watching the skinny lad disappear across the field. Then he smiled wryly and went back to his work.

All that summer Bali watched Reese closely, and, subtly, lest he make the sensitive youngster shy off, he began teaching Reese some of the fine points of the game. Reese's play, already skillful, became inspired. By the time the summer had waned and the baseball season had given way to football, Pee Wee had become the talk of the park.

The following spring, despite Reese's protestations, Bali took Pee Wee by the hand and led him to Ralph Kimmel, coach of the DuPont High baseball team.

"Mr. Kimmel," Bali said determinedly, "this boy wants to try out for the baseball team."

Coach Kimmel looked down at the brown-haired seventeen-year-old. Pee Wee, scarcely one hundred ten pounds. But whatever the coach might have been thinking, he knew boys.

"What about it, son?" he said soberly to Pee Wee. "You think you can make the team?"

Pee Wee shifted his feet uneasily. "I play for the New Covenant Church team."

The coach nodded. "They're a real good ball club."

Reese was encouraged. "I'd like to try out, anyway, Mr. Kimmel. If you think I've got a chance."

"We'll see soon enough," said the coach. "Get out on the field. By the way," he called after Reese, already racing to his position, "where do you play?"

"Second base," returned Pee Wee over his shoulder, never stopping, for fear the coach would change his mind.

And Pee Wee did play second base. He was, in truth, no ball of fire, but he was well on his way toward becoming the regular second baseman when he was spiked on the hand. So after appearing in three games, Reese's high school baseball career was finished.

There was enough of it, however, to keep the fire of hope burning in Pee Wee and to cause his parents' hearts to swell with pride. And besides, Pee Wee had earned his letter. He wore it like a badge of honor, that big letter *D*, on a wool sweater. He wouldn't take the garment off no matter what, but wore it all that winter. The letter covered most of his chest, so that his body appeared to be just a big letter *D* on a pair of legs as he stalked around the streets of Louisville.

But that letter, that proud, beautiful letter, was soon to bring Pee Wee to one of the darkest moments of his young life.

One fall day before his graduation, he wore the sweater to a DuPont football game. He was standing on the sidelines cheering his schoolmates on, feeling more a part of things than he had ever felt before in his life. Just then a couple of DuPont alumni walked up to him. They were former football players, tall and powerful looking.

One of them nudged the other and pointed to the letter on Reese's chest. "Hey, kid," he said to Pee Wee. "What'd you do to get a letter, play on the chess team?" Then both men roared with laughter.

Reese blushed furiously. He looked down at his shoe tops. "No," he said, his voice barely above a whisper. "I played baseball."

The fellow who had first spoken held his hands to his head in mock horror. "Holy cow!" he yelled. "They let any runt play ball these days."

Reese bit his lip to hold back the tears. He felt ashamed and humiliated, and he turned and walked away. His feet scuffed at the crackling leaves that lay red and gold on the sidewalk. He walked more slowly now, his hands in his pockets, the cheering and the music from the stadium growing dimmer in his ears. He stopped as a shout went up, and his heart beat faster momentarily. Then he walked on and a great sigh escaped his lips. "Who am I kidding?" he said to himself. "I'll never be a ballplayer. I don't even look like one."

CHAPTER 4

The painful memory of that embarrassing incident at the football game remained with Pee Wee for a long time. Nevertheless, when spring came to Louisville in 1937 he was back in uniform with the New Covenant Church team. Reese loved baseball—if they wanted to get him out they'd have to throw him out.

It was just a week-end game to him, though, for he had graduated from high school, and the time had come to help earn his way in the family. A relative got him a job with the Southern Bell Telephone Company as a cable splicer. It did wonders for Pee Wee. He was up and down telephone poles all day, like a squirrel. By the time the baseball season had gotten under way the exercise had added inches of muscle to Pee Wee's shoulders and legs, added solid pounds to his skinny frame. He still weighed only one hundred forty but he added four inches in height and was as solid as one of his telephone poles.

Keith Sparks, manager of the New Covenant team, was happy and surprised at the physical change in Reese. The wise pilot shifted Pee Wee to the shortstop slot soon after the season opened, where his now-powerful throwing arm would be of most value.

Reese was a new man. With his added strength he found new determination and new confidence. He burned up the amateur league that season and led his team to the city's amateur championship.

Before the day of the final play-off game, manager Sparks paid a visit to Cap Neal, then owner-manager of the Louisville Colonels. "Cap," he said, "I got a boy for you to look at."

Neal looked up at Sparks. "What's he play?"

"A whale of a shortstop."

Neal shook his head. "Not looking for one right now, Sparks."

But Sparks wasn't to be shaken off that easily. "Isn't Ray French just about ready to call it a day, Cap?"

Neal grunted, "Maybe, but we've got three or four good boys ready if French can't hold his job. Kids with good Class D experience, Sparks. Not New Covenant kids."

"I don't care who they are," Sparks returned. "They couldn't carry my boy's glove."

Neal looked up at Sparks curiously. The New Covenant manager was no blowhard, Neal knew. And he was a pretty fair judge of a kid's capabilities. Maybe he's got something, he thought.

"You sound pretty sold on this kid," Neal said.

Sparks nodded. "We're playing the last play-off game in your park tomorrow, Cap," he said. "Come around and take a look for yourself. Then you can buy me a box of cigars for tipping you off."

Neal drummed his fingers on the desk. He thought a minute, then he shrugged. "Maybe I will, Sparks. Maybe I will."

The New Covenant pilot grinned with satisfaction the next day when he saw Cap Neal take a seat behind his team's dugout. But he didn't say a word to Pee Wee about the Louisville manager's presence. Better not put pressure on the boy, Sparks thought. He might get jittery. Now if he'll only have a good day today. . . .

A roar from the crowd brought Sparks's head up. The first batter for the New Covenant team had rapped a single and the game was on. Pee Wee popped out his first time up, but in the third inning he made a great stop of a smash up the middle, flipped to second to start a double play. Sparks turned around and looked at Cap Neal. The Colonel's manager didn't blink an eye.

In the fifth inning Reese cracked a single to left. On the first pitch to the next batter he streaked for second and stole the bag well ahead of the catcher's throw. Sparks turned around again. Neal just shrugged.

In the sixth an opposing batter looped a little fly into left. Reese turned his back on the plate, scampered back, then at the last minute turned his head and caught the ball over his shoulder on the dead run. The stands resounded with applause as Reese trotted back to his position. Again Sparks turned around to look at Neal. The Colonels' manager was leaning forward on the railing now, looking keenly out at the field.

In the eighth inning Pee Wee came up again. He took the first pitch, then boomed a tremendous two-base hit off the left field wall. He pulled into second standing, and Neal's eyes were glinting now. When the game was over and the championship wrapped up for the New Covenant team, Neal walked over to Keith Sparks.

"Bring that Reese kid into my office next week, Sparks. And tell him to bring his father with him. We'll need his signature on a contract."

As city amateur champions, the New Covenant team

had won a trip to the World Series in New York. It was the New York Giants against the Yankees in the 1937 fall classic, and the kids from Louisville were bug eyed at the vast expanses of the ball parks. Here were all their heroes—Carl Hubbell, Lefty Gomez, Mel Ott and Bill Dickey and the rest. Before the first game Pee Wee managed to get Mel Ott's autograph on his score card, and when his friends teased him by hiding his treasure, he was ready to clean up the ball park with them until they returned it.

If you had told Pee Wee that afternoon that in three short years he'd be playing his heart out against the Giants as a member of the Brooklyn Dodgers, he'd have said you were crazy.

When the series was over, Pee Wee, Carl Reese and Keith Sparks gathered in Cap Neal's office. Pee Wee was all for signing quick and getting out before Neal changed his mind. But Sparks, unknown to the Reeses or Cap Neal, had another offer from Baltimore in his pocket, and he advised bargaining.

"How much?" he said crisply to Neal when the manager brought out the contract.

"Oh, a fair figure," drawled Neal.

"How much?" repeated Sparks.

"Sixty-five dollars a month."

Pee Wee started forward to grab the pen, but Sparks put out his arm to check him.

"I thought you were interested in signing this boy?" he said to Neal. "I guess I was wrong."

"Now, wait a minute, Sparks. That was a fair offer. After all, it isn't like Reese here has had a couple of seasons of pro ball behind him. A boy needs seasoning.

Yes, just like a good steak before it's ready. I'm taking your boy here on cold. It's a big opportunity for him."

"At one hundred dollars a month, Cap, or no deal. And a bonus of two hundred for signing."

Pee Wee looked at Sparks in amazement. But he said nothing.

Neal sighed. He drew a blank contract from his desk drawer. "I better say okay before you ask for a piece of the Colonels, too."

Sparks grinned. "I was just coming to that."

Neal's hand, reaching for the pen, stopped in mid-air. Pee Wee's mouth popped open.

"We'd like a clause in the contract, Neal, giving Reese five per cent of the purchase price when you sell his contract to a major league club."

Now Neal's jaw popped open. "You're going too far, Sparks. Anyway, what makes you think this kid's ever going to make a major league club?"

Sparks nodded. "He will. And you know as well as I do that such clauses are getting to be customary in minor league contracts, Cap. It's only fair that a kid share in the profit made on a deal involving him."

Neal sat there a moment, rubbing his jaw, thinking. Then he stood up. "Wait here a minute," he said to the three men. "I'll be right back."

As soon as he left the room Pee Wee, his father and Keith Sparks began jabbering at once. "Whoa, Whoa!" Sparks called finally. "Now don't you worry, Neal isn't going to throw us out. He'll give us what we want, all right. He just doesn't want to make it look too easy, that's all."

Neal strode back in, walked around his desk and sat

down. "I'm crazy and so's everybody else around here, but you've got yourself a deal." When the papers had been signed, he turned to Pee Wee. "Keep yourself in shape over the winter, son," he said. Then to Sparks, "You sure you're not descended from Jesse James?" But he laughed and shook hands with the New Covenant manager.

The Reese family whooped with joy when Pee Wee and his father returned with the news of his signing. Friends and neighbors kept dropping by for weeks afterward, offering their congratulations and best wishes. Except one member of the Reese clan. That was the relative who had wangled Pee Wee the job with the telephone company. "You're making a big mistake," he cautioned Reese one night. "You're out of your mind quitting your job to play with the Colonels. You've got a great future ahead of you with the telephone company. Ballplayers, bah! They're only good for a couple of years, then— nothing."

Pee Wee hesitated a minute, then he grinned and shook his head.

"I probably am nuts," he said, for he was still dazed by the suddenness of his good fortune. "But I'm going to take the chance. This is what I've wanted all my life. I know that I can make good in the big time!"

The Louisville hurler tugged at the peak of his cap and looked down at his battery mate. The big crowd at the Colonels' park was in a frenzy. It was tie score, top of the eighth, and St. Paul had runners on first and third with two out.

The Colonels' pitcher stretched, took a look back at the

runners, then delivered to the plate. The batter swung, cracked the ball sharply to the left side. Pee Wee Reese scampered over, scooped up the ball—then dropped it! By the time he recovered the batter was across first base and the runner from third had scored the tie-breaking run! Reese kicked at the dirt angrily as he went back to position. The next batter struck out. But the damage had been done. The game went to St. Paul.

In the Louisville clubhouse later, Pee Wee sat morosely in front of his locker, still in his sweat-stained uniform. Cap Neal walked by the young shortstop, deliberately casual, and punched him lightly on the shoulder. "Don't let it get you, kid," he said to Pee Wee. "Tomorrow's another day."

But tomorrow was no different. Reese kicked away an easy grounder and threw wildly to first, letting in two runs. The next day he threw one over the first baseman's head into the stands. Trying too hard to make good before the home town fans, he was pressing. And the more he erred, the more jittery he became. He couldn't eat, couldn't sleep. His parents wisely refrained from discussing baseball with him. Manager Cap Neal, too, maintained a tight-lipped silence. He was, however, beginning to get a little anxious about his shortstop.

Pee Wee was ready to go to pieces after his terrible start. Fortunately, the Colonels were scheduled for a road trip after the opening series at home. This saved Reese's baseball life.

Playing before a strange crowd away from home and with the pressure off his shoulders, Pee Wee began to settle down. By the time the Colonels returned home again Pee Wee had established himself as a shortstop to watch. An inner drive had taken hold of him, as if he had suddenly realized that what he had barely dared to dream was coming true. And he set out to prove he could really be a professional baseball player.

Whenever the Louisville Colonels were in town, the entire Reese family turned out to cheer their Pee Wee. And Reese no longer let them down. He grabbed everything hit his way with sure hands; his throws were accurate. At bat his specialty was booming doubles off the left field wall. He played sensationally and the entire club respected their new star.

The Colonels had a weak team that year; they weren't going anyplace. But Pee Wee played as if the pennant hung on every pitch. Before the season ended, his salary was raised to two hundred dollars a month, and scouts from the major leagues were beginning to drop around to watch Reese, the new star of the American Association.

Reese wound up the 1938 season hitting .279, including twenty-one doubles, and with one of the top fielding percentages in the league. For Carl Reese, Pee Wee's father, sitting in the stands almost daily to watch his son play, it was the happiest year of his life. It was also his last. Carl Reese died that winter. So for Pee Wee, baseball became more than just a game; it was a matter of economics. The family needed his help.

Several major league baseball clubs were also getting the idea that they could use Pee Wee's help. Three scouts had been on Reese's trail that season—Billy Evans, farm director for the Boston Red Sox, Clarence Rowland of the Chicago Cubs and Ted McGrew of the Brooklyn Dodgers. Evans, for one, had practically set up camp at the Louisville club that season, in order to watch Reese in action. When the baseball season ended, the intricate business machinery of the major leagues went into action.

Billy Evans walked into Cap Neal's office one day and came right to the point. "Cap," he said to the Colonels' owner, "I'd like to make a deal with you for Pee Wee Reese."

Neal had been expecting the offer for months. And he knew what he was going to do. "You know, Evans," he said to the Red Sox scout, "the Red Sox aren't the only ones interested in this kid."

Evans nodded. "I think I can beat anybody's offer."

"Could be," Neal returned. "How badly do you want Reese?"

"I won't kid you, Neal," Evans said. "Cronin doesn't have too many years left. One, maybe two. I think this kid's a great prospect. Within reason, I'd do most anything to get him."

"Even buy the whole Louisville ball club?"

Evans looked up sharply. "I don't think I heard you right, Neal."

The Colonels' boss grinned broadly. "It's not as crazy as it sounds, Evans." He leaned across his desk. "Seriously, here's the way I see it. I haven't been feeling too well lately. I've got to slow down. I'd like to sell my club, take it easy, go fishing someplace. Reese is an important asset to the Colonels. Naturally, whoever buys the team would want Reese along with it. So I don't know that I'd want to deal him off to anybody, unless the rest of the club went with the deal. Buy the Louisville club and you get Reese."

Evans looked skeptical. "It's a big order. I don't know if Yawkey'll go for the idea."

"He'll go for it if you go for it," Neal said. "What do you think of the idea, anyway?"

Evans thought for a minute. "I like it," he snapped.

Red Sox owner Tom Yawkey thought Evans had lost his mind when Billy first came to him with Neal's proposition. But Evans gradually swung him around to the idea that buying the Louisville club would be a sound investment in the long run. And besides, that was the only way they'd be sure of getting Pee Wee Reese. Yawkey finally agreed to the deal, taking in Frank McKinney and Donie Bush as partners.

The new owners of the Colonels met Pee Wee that winter, at contract time. Bush, acting as president and field manager, McKinney, treasurer, and Bruce Dudley, executive manager, had been biting their pencils to the nub trying to figure a budget for the 1939 season. Things didn't look too good. Now here was Pee Wee Reese waiting in the outer office, probably ready to ask for a fat raise. And with good reason, too.

"He deserves a lot more, but we can't afford to give him much above what he got last year," McKinney said. The others nodded their agreement. "Donie," McKinney said to Bush, "how about going outside and softening Reese up a little before we sit down with him and talk money?"

"Good idea," Bush agreed. He rose and left the office to greet Pee Wee outside. He returned in five minutes, beaming.

"What are you looking so happy about?" asked Dudley. "Did Reese volunteer to take a salary cut or something?"

Bush waved his arm expansively. "That's a nice boy, there, that Reese. We were just sitting and talking, and before you knew it we had come to terms for next year."

McKinney cocked his head suspiciously. "Yeah? For how much?" "Twice what he was getting last season."

McKinney and Dudley leaped from their chairs together.

"What!" they chorused. "That's fifty dollars a month more than you planned on giving him, just a few months ago."

"Well," Bush explained, "when I was a kid I'd have been tickled silly if somebody paid me that much. Besides," he smiled, "he called me mister. I like that in a youngster."

CHAPTER **5**

From Arcadia, Florida, the Colonels' spring training camp, to Sarasota, Florida, the Red Sox training camp, was not a long trip measured in miles. But Pee Wee Reese never made it. Instead, Boston manager Joe Cronin came over to the Colonels' camp to take a look at Pee Wee, and he went back to the Red Sox camp alone.

Maybe, as some baseball men have said, it was a mistake sending Cronin over to appraise Pee Wee who, after all, was being groomed to take Cronin's place at shortstop. In Cronin's favor, it turned out that Pee Wee—though no one knew it at the time—had just recovered from a siege of the flu and didn't look his best when spring training opened.

In any case, Cronin brought back a negative report on Reese to the Red Sox's owners. "The kid won't do," he told them. "I'm still good for a couple of years. Better years, I'm sure, than Reese can give you. Maybe by then you can line up somebody else to take my place."

Billy Evans, who was so high on Pee Wee, objected violently when Boston decided to sell Reese either to Chicago or Brooklyn. "You're crazy if you let him out of your hands!" he stormed. "I got you to shell out one hundred ninety-five thousand dollars for Louisville just to get that kid. You think I'd do it if he weren't worth it—and more?

Mark my words, this boy's going to be one of the best shortstops in the game a couple of years from now!"

Evans, however, lost the argument and also his job as farm director for the Red Sox. And Pee Wee stayed another year with Louisville, burning up the league.

The Colonels came alive in 1939, and led by the rampaging Reese they drove to a pennant. Pee Wee was never among the leaders in averages. But though he hit only .272 for the year, he hit in the clutch. A reputation that still rides with him began to blossom that year. "In a tight spot, when the big hit is needed, Reese is one of the most dangerous batters in the game," the writers were saying.

With his great speed, Pee Wee racked up twenty-two doubles that year. And he had picked up a new trick that endeared him to Louisville fans, who flocked to the park to watch the popular shortstop play. He had learned to hit to right, and his specialty was slicing outside pitches down the right field line and hotfooting around the bases for a triple. He whacked eighteen three-baggers in 1939, leading the American Association in that department.

On the base paths, Pee Wee drove opposing pitchers and catchers wild trying to nail him. He was fast; but more than that, he was smart. He was almost never cut down stretching a hit, and only once all year was he caught stealing. He stole thirty-five bases that year, too!

The big league scouts camped on Pee Wee's trail again. But while they were at it, Reese had done a little scouting on his own—of a different kind.

It was hot that July morning, hot even for Louisville. Pee Wee, as was his custom, was visiting one of his married sisters. He still had a couple of hours before he had to be out at the park for practice. While his sister was getting up a snack for lunch, Pee Wee strolled out into the back yard.

There was a low fence, overgrown with ivy and rosebushes, separating his sister's yard from her neighbor's. Pee Wee wandered aimlessly around, breathing in the heady, flower-scented air of the beautiful morning. He plucked a rose from the bush on the fence, then glanced into the yard next door.

Sitting cross legged on a beach chair, the sun glinting on her dark hair, was one of the most beautiful girls he had ever seen. He stood there and watched her for a moment as she turned her head to catch the full rays of the warm sun on her drying hair. When she looked up and saw him she smiled, and Pee Wee felt a strange flutter in his heart.

"Hi," she said.

Pee Wee nodded. He was too nervous even to answer.

"I'm Dorothy Walton," she went on. "Who are you?"

Reese's thoughts raced wildly. He was so flustered by this lovely girl he didn't know what to say. He was afraid to appear fresh or foolish in her eyes. He gestured futilely toward his sister's house. "She's, ah, I'm . . . ah . . . my name is Harold," he managed to blurt out. "Yes, that's right, I'm Harold Reese." He said it with a kind of pride, as if it were an accomplishment for him to have said something coherent in the face of such disconcerting beauty.

The girl laughed and little lights danced in her eyes. Pee Wee was sunk, right there and then. He blushed to the roots of his hair, murmured something that sounded like an apology and fled back to the safety of his sister's house.

But the next morning Pee Wee was back again at his sister's. He walked into the yard, half hoping yet half afraid he would again see the beautiful Dorothy Walton. The yard next door was empty. Pee Wee felt a pang of disappointment. He wondered at it, this strange new feeling. He walked around the yard, looked at the flowers, inspected the shrubbery, yet all the time seeing nothing. His mind was next door.

Dorothy, meanwhile, had seen Pee Wee arrive. The day before, she, too, had felt that uncertain flutter of the heart. The innocent-faced Pee Wee with his hesitant, boyish smile, had attracted her immensely.

She dashed about her house now, excited, seeking an excuse to go out into the yard.

"Whatever is the matter with you, Dorothy?" asked Mrs. Walton, watching her daughter dash from room to room. "What is all this sudden fluttering about?"

"It's that boy from next door, Mother. The one I was telling you about yesterday. He's back!"

"Well, go outside and say hello to the young man, if that's the way you feel about it."

"Mother! I can't go outside . . . just like that, without a reason." Dorothy explained. "Don't we have some garbage around or something I can take out?"

"I'm afraid we're fresh out of garbage, dear," Mrs. Walton said, suppressing a smile. "But maybe we can round up some old newspapers for you to take out."

Thus was their romance over the back fence resumed. But the path of true love, of course, never runs smooth. Pee Wee was off on a road trip soon after their first meeting. When he returned, the Waltons' had moved to another part of town.

Pee Wee, visiting his sister again, mooned about the yard, looking as if he had lost his best friend.

"Why don't you go over and visit her?" his sister asked, appearing suddenly behind Pee Wee.

Reese whirled around, sputtering with embarrassment. "Who? What? Visit who? What are you talking about?"

"Now don't try to kid me, Harold Reese," his sister scolded. But her eyes were laughing. "You know darn well I mean Dorothy Walton."

"Who?" Pee Wee said, pretending to be puzzled. "Oh, you mean that girl who used to live next door? What do I want to visit her for?" he shrugged innocently.

"I guess I made a mistake, then. I thought you were interested in her," his sister said, turning and going back into the house.

"Not me. Uh, by the way, where did she move?" Reese said with deliberate casualness. "I think one of the guys on the team would like to meet her."

"Naturally," his sister returned, with a straight face. "Come inside. I have her address written on a piece of paper."

Pee Wee made his first official appearance at the Walton home that same night. He was scared out of his wits, but it was a move born of desperation. He had to see Dorothy again. And every night the team was home was date night for the two of them from then on. One such evening Pee Wee and Dorothy were furiously engaged in a ping-pong game, when Dorothy's little brother came down the stairs to size up his sister's new boy friend.

The youngster's eyes bugged when he spotted Pee Wee. He scrambled up the stairs and made some excuse to call his sister.

"Hey, sis!" he said, the awe apparent in his voice. "Why didn't you tell me who you were goin' out with? Boy!"

"Why? Who is he?" Dorothy asked, puzzled by her brother's tone.

"You mean you don't know! He's Pee Wee Reese of the Louisville Colonels!"

"Really?" said Dorothy calmly. "That's nice."

Fortunately, Pee Wee didn't let the flush of romance affect his play on the baseball field. Coolly and brilliantly, he was leading the Colonels to the American Association flag and eventual triumph in the Little World Series.

Before the month of July was over, however, Pee Wee was head over heels in love—and headed for the major leagues.

Long Island Sound lay blue and sparkling in the July sun, the calm waters lapping gently against the sides of the sleek white and tan cabin cruiser moving slowly along the shore. A dozen or so sport-shirted men milled aimlessly about the deck or sprawled lazily in camp chairs munching sandwiches.

"Yessir," one of the loungers remarked, "Larry Mac-Phail has picked some funny places for press conferences before. But this takes the cake," he said, waving his hand at the luxurious trappings of the cruiser.

"I can think of worse places," said another.

"Okay, let's go," called a third sports writer, walking over to the group. "Earn your keep. Larry has a few words to say to us."

"Hah! Now the rest of the afternoon's shot," came the crack. "From Larry's few words I could write nine columns."

"Yeah, and sometimes they sound like it," came the retort.

Further witticisms were cut off by the appearance of the host himself, Larry MacPhail, executive vice-president of the Brooklyn Dodgers, turned out resplendently in white flannel slacks, dark blue jacket and a yachting cap.

"H'ya, fellas," he greeted the sports writers. "There's a couple of things I wanted to mention to you fellas today. One of them's pretty big, so I'll get to that first."

MacPhail took a sheaf of papers from his inside jacket pocket. "I have here," he said to the assembled sports writers, "a four-page letter from scout Ted McGrew. You boys all know Ted."

The writers murmured assent. They all knew and liked the popular, rotund scout for the Brooklyn club.

"I got this a little over a week ago. It's all about a young kid with the Louisville Colonels that Ted's stuck on. The only thing is, Ted said, the kid can't hit a low outside curve."

The writers stood quietly, waiting for MacPhail to come to the point.

"A couple of days later, I get a telegram from Ted," MacPhail said, pulling the message from his pocket. "It says: 'Just saw Reese hit two outside curves against the right field wall for triples. And he still runs bases like Cobb.'" MacPhail folded the message and returned it to his pocket.

"Well," MacPhail went on, smiling, "I thought for a while there old Ted had gone overboard on this boy. Run bases like Cobb." He paused and the writers laughed politely.

"So I sent Andy High down to check on McGrew's

reports on the kid. Andy was even higher on him than McGrew. 'Larry boy,' I said, 'this you got to see for yourself.' Well I've just returned from Louisville, gentlemen, and I tell you this Reese is the greatest prospect I've ever seen. Furthermore, I think this kid could mean the pennant for Brooklyn. Not this year—but mark my words, in a couple of years, Reese will make us a winner."

"He must be some punkins, Larry," said one of the writers. "What does he play?"

"Shortstop," MacPhail said tersely.

The writers looked at one another significantly. The regular shortstop for the Brooklyn Dodgers then was their fiery manager—Leo "The Lip" Durocher. This Reese better be good!

One week later the Dodger club announced the purchase of Pee Wee Reese for forty thousand dollars and four players. Reese was kind of expecting that he'd be sold to a major league team before the 1939 season ended. He was sitting in a Pullman car, returning to Louisville after the American Association All-Star game, when he got the news.

A newspaperman, who came upon Reese sitting in the car, broke it to him. "Congratulations, Pee Wee," he said, sticking out his hand.

Reese shook the proffered hand. "Thanks, but what happened? I win the Irish sweepstakes or something?"

The newspaperman grinned. "Just about. I heard you've just been sold to the Brooklyn Dodgers."

Reese looked stunned. "Brooklyn!" he wailed. "No! I don't want to go to Brooklyn!"

CHAPTER **6**

There was an air of hopefulness in the Dodgers' 1940 training camp at Clearwater, Florida. Under the flamboyant, but always skillful, leadership of Larry MacPhail in the front office and Leo Durocher on the field, the Dodgers had finished third the year before and were being spoken of as the most exciting team in the league.

MacPhail, brash, confident and extremely vocal—Dodger traveling secretary John McDonald called him "the Living Loudspeaker"—had brought a new order to Brooklyn. Taking over the helm in 1938, he had reorganized the club from top to bottom, all the way to the usher and special police staffs at Ebbets Field. He took over a crumbling franchise, spent money, traded shrewdly and began building an organization that still stands as one of the most powerful in the major leagues.

Many baseball writers, referring to MacPhail's explosive, unpredictable personality, jocularly called his regime the Reign of Terror. In a way it was just that. But it paid off where it counted—in the National League standings and in the cash register.

During his first year at Brooklyn he introduced night baseball, radio broadcasts and Dolph Camilli to the citizens of Flatbush. The Dodgers finished seventh. But MacPhail had barely begun to fight.

In 1939 MacPhail dealt for Whitlow Wyatt, Hugh Casey and Dixie Walker, who were destined to become famous names in Brooklyn. And he made Leo Durocher manager of the Dodgers. Leo was every bit as brash, confident and loud as MacPhail, and together they wrote some of the most colorful chapters in Brooklyn Dodger history.

And now, in the early spring of 1940, there were two rookies named Harold in camp whom the Dodgers hoped could help bring Brooklyn a pennant. They were Harold Pee Wee Reese, and Harold Reiser, called "Pistol Pete" because of his fondness for cowboy movies.

Pee Wee wasn't long in meeting up with the oddities of working for the Brooklyn Dodgers. He reported to Clearwater a week later than anybody else, simply because he had received three letters from the club during the winter, each informing him of a different reporting date. A siege of flu had again hit Pee Wee, and when he finally did make it to the training camp he was thin and pale.

His arrival at Clearwater was much heralded, and the skeptical writers were on hand to give the youngster from Louisville the critical eye.

Reese's first emergence from the Dodger clubhouse caused an epidemic of raised eyebrows among the assembled writers. He looked more like a substitute bat boy than a sensational rookie prospect. His uniform hung limply on his thin frame, his boyish face was wan and he looked scared to death.

Once out on the playing field, however, Pee Wee asserted himself. After he had handled a dozen or so ground balls batted down to him by the batting coach, scout Ted McGrew, his loudest booster, strolled over to the sports writers.

"What do you think of the kid?" he asked.

"Hands like a pickpocket," said one.

McGrew beamed and nodded his agreement.

"But tell me, Ted," said Eddie Murphy of the now-defunct New York *Sun,* "why's he so pale?"

"Well heck," protested McGrew, "the kid's only been in Florida a couple of days!"

"Where'd he spend the winter?" Murphy asked, giving McGrew the needle. "In jail?"

"Aw, you guys," said McGrew, but he knew the writers were only kidding him.

"What's up, Ted?" asked Leo Durocher, coming over to the group. "These loafers giving you a hard time? We'll bar 'em from the swimming pool and make 'em do an honest day's work for a change."

"We were just looking over the wonder boy from Louisville, Leo," one of the writers said. "He handles himself pretty good out there. But you sure he's twenty? He don't look old enough to shave."

"We're not paying him to shave," Durocher growled. "I don't care if he eats lollipops after lunch and likes oatmeal for breakfast. If he's half as good as McGrew says he is, he's playing shortstop for me."

Durocher looked out at the playing field. "Hey, Cookie!" he called to third baseman Lavagetto, taking his turn in the batting cage, "hit a couple down to short."

Lavagetto choked up on his bat and rapped a couple of sharp grasscutters out toward Pee Wee. Reese glided over smoothly, stabbed the grounders and flipped to first in one easy motion.

"That's enough for me," Durocher said, turning away and walking back to the sports writers. "That kid can play shortstop on any team."

"Come on now, Leo," a writer scoffed. "Just two easy ground balls—and you're making this kid your shortstop already?"

Durocher shook his head. "Two balls or two dozen, it makes no difference. You can tell. You watch the way a kid moves after a ball, the way he gloves it and the way he gets it over to the first baseman. You can tell like that whether he's a shortstop or a bum. This kid," he said, jerking his thumb over his shoulder, "this kid is a shortstop, a great shortstop."

"We'll record your words for posterity, Leo," a writer said, making a note on a sheet of yellow paper. "Let's hope they stand up."

"They will," Durocher snapped, "or I'll eat 'em, and your typewriter, too."

Durocher was really convinced, after that brief look, and the sharp note of sincerity in his voice half convinced the professionally skeptical writers. Unfortunately for the harmony of the club, however, the Dodger manager would find he couldn't convince one man that easily— Larry MacPhail.

The spring of 1940 was a bitterly cold one in Florida. Everybody on the Dodger team was freezing through the early exhibition games. Everybody, that is, except Pee Wee Reese. Pee Wee was hot. His fielding was a revelation. And at bat, the one spot Durocher was a little uneasy about, they couldn't get him out. He was smashing the ball at a better than .400 clip during the exhibition games.

He broke up game after game with a timely hit, ran the bases like a deer and stole opposing catchers frantic. And all the while Durocher watched him from the bench, his eyes glowing. He was seeing another Leo Durocher out there, playing the way he had always played—except for that little extra push, that aggressiveness, that holler.

The morning before an exhibition game with Boston, Durocher called Pee Wee to one side in the clubhouse. He draped an arm around the youngster's shoulder in friendly fashion and led him into his office.

"Pee Wee," he said to Reese, "I've been watching you out there. And I like what I see. You're a shortstop. I knew it the first time I saw you field a grounder down in Sarasota. And I told everybody what I thought. You're hitting, too. I always liked the way you stood up there and took your cut, but I don't mind telling you we were a little worried about your hitting. We're not any more. You'll carry your weight at the plate."

"Well, thanks, Mr. Durocher," Pee Wee said, pleased by this unusual outburst from his manager.

Durocher waved his hand deprecatingly. "Never mind the thanks. Just keep playing the way you are, that'll be my thanks. But there are a couple of things, Pee Wee. I want you to get a little more fire in your play. I want you to take charge out there. Take my place, be the holler guy, keep the infield on its toes."

"But Mr. Durocher . . ." Pee Wee shook his head bewildered.

"Never mind the buts." Durocher walked over to Pee Wee and stuck his finger at him. "Listen. When opening day comes, you're going to be out at shortstop. And you're going to stay out there. I can't do it any more. I'm depending on you to do it for me." Durocher strode to the door of his office. "That's it, kid. Keep it in mind. You're my boy out there."

Pee Wee sat in his chair a long time after the door had slammed behind Durocher. He sat and thought, overwhelmed and, yes, a little frightened by what Durocher had told him. Take charge of the infield? Be the holler guy? Me? Pee Wee Reese—with only two years of baseball behind me? Oh, it was okay for Durocher to come up as a rookie with the Yankees and start shouting everyone down. I heard plenty about him. But not me.

How can I tell big stars like Dolph Camilli, Pete Coscarart and Lavagetto what to do, how to play? Why, they've been leading me around by the hand all spring, like the hick from Louisville that I am. I won't do it! Heck, I *can't* do it! I'll play the game with everything I've got, but I'm not going to tell these guys how to play.

So Reese thought, as he sat alone in Durocher's office, and felt for the first time the cold grip of anxiety knot his stomach. What's going to happen now? Will Durocher pull me out of the line-up if I don't take charge as he says? Pee Wee gnawed at his lips worriedly for a minute. Then he sighed deeply and went out on the playing field to take his practice.

Nobody ever worked harder to get a team off to a flying start than manager Leo Durocher did in 1940. When the opening gun sounded the Dodgers were hot, sweeping nine games in a row before being stopped. The streak tied a National League record that was to stand up until the Dodgers themselves surpassed it in 1955.

Everything seemed to be breaking right for the Dodgers

and Durocher. Everything, that is, except, the growing problem at shortstop.

After his great play in the spring, the major league jitters seemed to catch up with Pee Wee Reese. Once the games started to count in the standings, he tightened up—with disastrous results. He couldn't get his batting average above the .200 mark, and in the field he was simply booting himself right back to Louisville.

Day after day, Durocher sat on the bench and watched his young protégé fall apart. Every error the kid made, every feeble pop fly he hit, was like a knife in Durocher's ribs.

What to do, what to do? That was Leo's problem. Take the kid out of the line-up before he loses the pennant for us, or stick with him? But every time Durocher sat alone in his office before a game, drawing up the line-up, the memory of Miller Huggins came back to him.

When Durocher had come with the Yankees as a swaggering rookie with a big mouth, it was manager Miller Huggins' faith that kept him in the majors after everybody else tried to run him out of baseball altogether. It was Huggins that Leo tried to emulate as a manager. And he knew what Huggins would have done in the case of Pee Wee Reese. So Pee Wee stayed in the line-up another day and still another.

Larry MacPhail, however, had no such memories to guide him—just the league standings and the horrible statistics telling the tale of Reese's playing. He called Durocher into his office early one morning and lit into Leo for his laxness with Reese.

MacPhail wasn't one to waste time with greetings.

"You're playing shortstop, today, Leo," he said to Durocher.

Leo lifted his eyebrows. "Why, Larry? What's wrong with Reese?"

"What's wrong with Reese?" MacPhail fumed. "Where are you every day, in the Polo Grounds? The kid's not playing ball out there. Get him out of the line-up—today!"

Durocher raised his hand to halt the tirade. "Keep your shirt on, Larry," he soothed. "All right, I'll admit he's looked bad the past couple of days. But give him a chance, he'll work out of it. He was great in spring training."

"I don't care if he hit .900 in spring training and fielded like a magician. I'm talking about now, you understand, Leo? Now!"

"But Larry, the kid's real good! Give him a chance," Durocher protested.

"He'll get his chance some other time," MacPhail shot back. "Right now I'm not paying you to collect splinters on the bench while he kicks away ball games. I want you to get out there and show me some of that sparkling fielding I used to read about in the papers," he jeered.

Durocher leaned his hands on MacPhail's desk and thrust his chin out belligerently. "I'm telling you this kid's too good to take out. He's staying in."

MacPhail slammed his fist on the desk. "And I'm telling you he's out! And you're in! Who needs you to manage, anyway? With the players I got you I could sit on the bench myself and manage this team into a pennant."

Durocher laughed. "What a joke! You manage!"

MacPhail's manner suddenly switched to one of icy

calm. He leveled his finger at Durocher. "I'm telling you for the last time, Leo," he said menacingly, "you're playing shortstop from now on."

Durocher caught the abrupt change of tone in MacPhail's voice. "What you mean, Larry, is that unless I take Reese out and play short myself, I'm fired. Is that it?"

"Now you're getting the pitch," said MacPhail.

Durocher turned angrily on his heel and stalked out of the room.

So Pee Wee was benched that afternoon, and Durocher went out to play shortstop. Reese was plunged into the depths of gloom by his failure, but he was keen minded enough to use his bench-warming time to watch—and learn.

Fortunately for Pee Wee—and in the long run for Brooklyn—Durocher's aging bones couldn't take the day-after-day play. On May 15th the Dodger pilot injured his arm in a game against the Reds, and Pee Wee again took over at shortstop.

Except for his wartime years in service, he's been there ever since.

It may very well have been that his two weeks on the bench served to acclimate Pee Wee to the climate of the major leagues, because when he broke back into the line-up he demonstrated immediately that he was back there to stay. His fielding steadied and he began to make plays that had the Dodger fans roaring with delight. His batting average climbed, too, and he hit safely in five straight games after his return to play.

On May 26th, with the Dodgers battling the Reds for league leadership, Pee Wee hit his first major league home run. And it was a memorable one. The Dodgers were locked in a 1–1 tie with the Phillies when Pee Wee came to bat in the tenth inning and stroked a line drive shot into the left field stands for a 2–1 victory. Victim of Reese's winning blast was Kirby Higbe, who was to become a Dodger himself the following year.

A week later, with the shortstop job apparently sewed up for Pee Wee, misfortune struck him a near-crippling blow. In the twelfth inning of a ball game with the Chicago Cubs, Pee Wee was beaned by a fast ball thrown by Jake Mooty. He spent a pain-racked week with a brain concussion in Chicago's Masonic Hospital, then for two weeks more he was riding the bench while the Dodgers speculated on the results of his accident.

There was no problem of permanent physical damage. The question was—would there be a mental block? Could this youngster, in his first year of major league baseball, come back off a beaning and play effectively again? Players more experienced than Pee Wee had been beaned and had failed to make a comeback. It was expected that he'd be somewhat plate shy, at least. But how much?

Pee Wee wasn't long in answering. He got back into the line-up on June 21st, against the Pittsburgh Pirates. All he did that day was slam out a single, a double and a triple in four times at bat before Durocher removed him in the sixth inning to rest him.

Nor did his hitting stop there. He hit safely in the next seven straight games, going thirty for twelve, an average of .400. Throughout the summer he ran up a streak of twenty-six straight games in which he got on base with either a walk or a hit. He was stopped for one day, then ran up another streak of twenty-two games before he was stopped again.

On July 3rd, Pee Wee hit his second major league home run, one which was important enough to endear him to the Dodger fans forever, had he never hit another one.

The Dodgers and the hated Giants were wrestling in a 3–3 tie at the Polo Grounds. The bases were loaded and up came Pee Wee. He promptly drove one of Hy Vandenberg's fast balls for a grand slam home run, winning the game, 7–3, and giving the Dodgers a one-game lead over the Cincinnati Reds.

On the Giant bench the next day, manager Bill Terry was groaning over Pee Wee's game-winning hit. "I don't know," said Terry, "whether or not Reese can hit enough to stick with Brooklyn. But I do know he knocked one of my pitchers right out of the major leagues. Vandenberg has been shipped down to Jersey City."

Reese's third homer came exactly one month later. He hit it in the ninth inning off Ken Raffensberger of the Cubs. It was the Dodgers' only run of the day as they lost, 2–1.

In the ninth inning the next day, Pee Wee pulled a losing game out of the fire with the fourth homer of his career. With the Dodgers behind by a run, he slammed one into the bleachers to tie the game, and in the eleventh Camilli homered to win it.

There was no doubt now about who was the Dodgers' shortstop. MacPhail still growled to Durocher often enough about his masterminding from the bench, but now Leo could point to Pee Wee's playing and hitting, and win the argument. Besides, the way Reese was playing, MacPhail would have been scalded in printers' ink by the writers had he tried to pull Pee Wee out.

What MacPhail couldn't do, however, hard luck did. On August 15th, Pee Wee broke a bone in the heel of his left foot while sliding into second. As they carried Reese off the field for the second time that season, Durocher saw the Dodger pennant going off with him. As far as Leo was concerned, Pee Wee was the backbone of the infield, an opinion echoed in the newspapers the next day.

When the medical report on Pee Wee indicated he was through for the rest of the year, the sports writers generally wrote off the Dodgers' pennant chances. And despite Durocher's determined efforts to keep the Dodgers in the race, they tailed off, finishing second, twelve games behind the Cincinnati Reds.

Pee Wee wound up the season with a respectable .272 average. But it was mainly his fielding skill that writers and baseball men talked about. Such hard-bitten critics as Bill Terry, Gabby Hartnett and Bill McKechnie called Pee Wee the rookie of the year. Despite his bad start and two crippling accidents, Pee Wee was in the major leagues to stay. Even MacPhail wouldn't have argued about that.

CHAPTER 7

You could feel it in the air of the Dodgers' Havana training camp that spring of 1941. This was it. This was the year the Dodgers and all of Brooklyn had been waiting twenty years for. The players, the fans, even the experts picked the Dodgers to win the pennant weeks before the training season opened.

There was good reason for the optimism, too. For all his brass and bluster, Larry MacPhail was a clever businessman who knew when to keep his affairs quiet. While most of the club owners were shuttling between Cincinnati and Detroit, watching the World Series of 1940, MacPhail was working on next year.

There were two players he wanted badly, pitcher Kirby Higbe of the Phillies and catcher Mickey Owen of the Cardinals. MacPhail knew he had to move carefully, for if either club got wind of the fact that he had gotten one of the men, they'd never give him the other. Besides, Horace Stoneham of the Giants was also after Higbe, and nothing would have delighted him more than to steal the pitcher from under MacPhail's nose.

Working quietly, therefore, MacPhail first obtained Higbe by seeking out Gerald Nugent, president of the Phillies, and offering him one hundred thousand dollars for the pitcher. Nugent almost fell out of his chair at the offer. He had hoped to get seventy-five thousand dollars at most. What he didn't know, of course, was that Mac-Phail would have given even more, just for the satisfaction of stealing Higbe from Stoneham.

Then, before news of the sale could be announced by the commissioner's office, MacPhail hustled over to Branch Rickey of the Cardinals. Instead of meeting him directly, however, MacPhail contrived to "run into him accidentally."

"Say, Branch," MacPhail tossed off casually, "How do you feel about selling me Owen?"

"I don't know, Larry," Rickey replied. "I'm not particularly eager to sell him. I like him myself."

"You probably like him more than I do," MacPhail returned easily. "I just figured I might take him off your hands if I could get him cheap."

Rickey's eyes narrowed. MacPhail's manner was almost too offhand to suit the cagey Cardinal executive. Suddenly the light dawned on Rickey. Or so he thought.

"By the way, Larry," he said, just as casually, "what's this I hear about the Phillies being willing to sell Higbe?"

MacPhail waved his arm. "Nugent's crazy!" he said. "You know what he wants for Higbe? A hundred thousand dollars!"

Rickey laughed. "Who'd be crazy enough to give one hundred thousand dollars for Higbe?"

MacPhail laughed, too. "Yeah, who?"

"So you're interested in Owen, eh, Larry?" Rickey asked.

"If the price is right."

"He'll come high."

"How high?" asked MacPhail.

Rickey thought for a minute. "You can have him for sixty thousand dollars and two players, one of them a catcher."

MacPhail stuck out his hand. "You got a deal."

With the addition of these two players, the Dodgers looked solid enough to beat anybody. Besides Higbe, they had Whitlow Wyatt, Curt Davis, Van Lingle Mungo, Freddie Fitzsimmons and Hugh Casey for the pitching staff. The outfield boasted Joe Medwick, Pete Reiser and Dixie Walker; the infield was the best in the league with the return of Reese, Lavagetto at third, Coscarart on second and Camilli on first.

After straining at the barrier all through the spring, the Dodgers opened the season with a loud thud. Their optimism was washed away practically overnight as they lost three straight to the Giants, and the Flatbush fans were up in arms.

The fans and the newspapers started riding Durocher and the Dodger players, but happily the team's fortunes soon reversed themselves. The Dodgers started winning. And MacPhail, to bolster his infield, bought Billy Herman from the Cubs to play second. Pete Coscarart simply couldn't keep pace with the rest of the infield. Too, Pee Wee Reese was beginning to look as if he could use a veteran hand like Herman to steady him. So Billy, who had also served his baseball apprenticeship with the New Covenant Church team, was brought on.

His presence didn't seem to help Pee Wee at all. Something seemed to have happened to him. The youngster was playing terrible ball, worse than he had early the season before.

Had it been any other year, things wouldn't have been

so bad. But this was the big year. Brooklyn was jumping. Every time the Dodgers returned from a road trip, the fans would be waiting at the airport or the railroad depot, and there'd be an ovation for the players.

But Reese didn't feel a part of it. He knew the other Dodgers were unsure of him, felt he might let them down. The players never said anything to Pee Wee, but he could see it in their looks, in the way conversation ceased when he approached a group of them in a hotel lobby or on the field. They couldn't hide their feelings that things would be better with a different shortstop. Maybe they didn't mean to hurt Pee Wee, but they did.

And actually, it did seem that every time Pee Wee made a bad play it cost the Dodgers a close ball game. And they were in a bitter battle for first place with the St. Louis Cardinals.

In one game with Cincinnati Pee Wee kicked a ground ball that let in the winning room in the ninth inning. Later, in the clubhouse, he sat morosely in front of his locker, his uniform still on, while the other players dressed silently and left the ball park.

Finally, Pee Wee undressed and stepped into the shower. In the safety of the running water, he let the tears run unchecked down his cheeks. Into the stall next to him stepped coach Red Corriden.

"Say, Pee Wee," Corriden called to Reese. "I understand your mom came up from Louisville today to watch you play."

Reese gulped back his sobs. "That's right, Red," he said.

"You know," said Corriden, who knew the agony Pee

Wee felt, "she must be feeling pretty bad about that error you made today."

Reese nodded miserably.

"You know how to make her feel better? When you meet her outside, give her the biggest smile you've got, like it was nothing at all that happened."

Pee Wee dressed hurriedly and rushed to meet his mother, that big, boyish smile on his face. And Corriden knew that Pee Wee would eventually come around.

But on May 21st, after the Dodgers had dropped their fourth straight game, Durocher announced he was benching Reese and taking over at shortstop himself. He had fought against it for weeks, but Pee Wee's prolonged batting slump—and finally a blunder the day before at shortstop—forced Durocher to make his move.

It was in the third inning against the Cubs, with two out and men on first and second. With Kirby Higbe pitching to Lou Stringer at the plate, Reese made a dash for second, as though expecting a pick-off throw from Higbe. But Higbe pitched—and Stringer promptly bounced a ground ball directly through the spot Pee Wee had just vacated. The runner from second and the Cub rally was kept alive.

"I don't know what Reese was thinking about when he ran for second," Durocher said after the game. "Ever since Higbe's been in the league I've never seen him try to pick a runner off second. He never throws to that bag when he's pitching. I think it's time to give Reese a rest."

When he was benched, Pee Wee had only two hits for his last seventeen times at bat.

Pee Wee didn't stay out of the line-up long, simply because Durocher couldn't play every day. But while the

Dodgers kept their lead in the tight pennant race, Reese kept bungling along. In a crucial game against the second-place Cardinals in August, Pee Wee made two errors in one inning to allow the Redbirds all their runs—enough to win and close up the gap to league leadership.

At last, on September 25th, the Dodgers clinched the pennant in Boston, Whitlow Wyatt shutting out the Braves, 6–0, while the Cardinals lost.

The train ride home from Boston was like a carnival, the players delirious with joy. They were mobbed by thousands of fans who met them at Grand Central station, cheering and grabbing them, ripping their clothes, carrying them on their backs. Amid the happy roistering, Pee Wee Reese stood with a little smile, happy, but feeling not quite a part of it all.

It had been a great year, a memorable year for Brooklyn and the Dodgers. But not for Pee Wee Reese. It was by far his worst year in baseball. He batted only .229. And he made forty-seven more errors than any other infielder in the league.

It's a phenomenon baseball observers and so-called experts have never been able to explain—the abrupt reversal of playing form by a baseball player, that is.

In the 1941 season, the Dodgers reached heights never before attained in twenty-one years by a Brooklyn team. They won the pennant. But through it all Pee Wee Reese played like a scared sandlotter. Then the World Series turned out to be a debacle for the Dodgers, as the New York Yankees made a shamble of their hopes. Yet almost alone through the deluge Pee Wee Reese, the young sophomore shortstop glittered at bat and in the field. He was the standout among all of the Dodgers and came through when the going was toughest.

The Dodgers went into the World Series as optimistically as they opened the season—and with as disastrous results. Brooklyn had won an even hundred games to grab the pennant. Whitlow Wyatt and Kirby Higbe each had won twenty-two. Pete Reiser, only twenty-two years old, was the youngest man ever to win the National League batting championship, hitting .343. Joe Medwick had hit .318 and Dixie Walker .311. Mickey Owen was strong behind the plate. The infield was in great shape. Well, almost in great shape. But maybe Reese wouldn't throw away too many balls.

Curt Davis opened the series for Brooklyn, against Red Ruffing for the Yankees. In the second inning Joe Gordon homered; in the fourth, Charlie Keller walked and scored on Bill Dickey's double. The Yankees went into the fifth inning leading, 2–0, and the Dodgers still hadn't reached Ruffing for even one hit.

Then Pee Wee took charge of things. First man up in the fifth, he rapped Ruffing's first offering for a sharp single to left. Owen followed with a triple and Reese scored the Dodgers' first run of the series.

The Yankees scored again in the sixth to make the score 3–1. Then Ruffing again clamped down on the Dodgers. And once more Reese shook the Yankee veteran loose. With two out in the seventh and Lavagetto on first as the result of an error, Pee Wee singled to left. Lavagetto held up at second, then scored a moment later as Rizzo singled. That was all the scoring for the day. The Dodgers lost it, 3–2. But the players began to look at Pee Wee with new respect.

It was Whitlow Wyatt, the Dodger ace, against Spud Chandler in the second game. The Yanks drew first blood again, scoring a run in the second on a single by Keller, a walk to Gordon and a single by Chandler. In the third they picked up another tally on a double by Henrich and a single by Keller.

The Dodgers stormed back in the fifth, with Reese in the middle of it. Camilli worked Chandler for a pass, Medwick doubled and Lavagetto walked, filling the bases. Reese, up next, ran the count to three and two, then rammed a vicious grasscutter through the mound past second base. But Gordon made a magnificent diving stop, flipped to second as he lay prone, then forced Lavagetto coming down from first. Pee Wee was robbed of his hit, but he batted in a run as Camilli scored easily from third. Owen then singled to score Medwick, and the score was tied.

The Dodgers scored their third run—the winning one as it turned out—in the sixth inning. Walker was safe on an error by Gordon, Herman singled to right, Camilli singled to right scoring Walker, and that was the ball game.

The way the Dodgers acted in the dressing room later —that was the World Series. "We've got 'em now," they yelled. "Wait till we get 'em over in Brooklyn! We'll murder the bums!"

They were laughing and singing in the showers, clapping each other on the back, doing everything but asking each other how they were going to spend their World Series money.

And Pee Wee, grinning and singing, felt as if a great load had been removed from his shoulders. In those first two games, he had shown that he could come through when even the veterans were being stopped cold, that he could rise to great heights when the pressure was on.

For Pee Wee and the Dodgers, however, that afternoon saw the last of the merrymaking in the Brooklyn club-house. The rest of the World Series was a nightmare.

In the third game Freddie Fitzsimmons and Marius Russo, the Yankees' young left-hander, were blazing along in a scoreless duel when Fate literally whacked the Dodgers in the shins. With two out in the seventh inning Russo shot a low line drive back at the box. The ball hit Fitzsimmons on the left leg and popped high in the air. Reese raced over from short, dove headlong and grabbed the ball for the third out. It was a sensational catch, and the crowd roared its approval.

But the cheers soon turned to groans. For Fitzsimmons, limping and cursing, was being helped from the field. The drive had crippled him. Hugh Casey warmed up hurriedly in the bull pen to face the Yankees in the eighth.

He got the first man, but that was all. Rolfe, Henrich, DiMaggio and Keller singled in succession, driving two runs in and Casey out of the game. Larry French relieved and got Bill Dickey to hit into a double play, but the damage had been done.

And it was Pee Wee, however, who at least saved the Dodgers the ignominy of a shutout. In their half of the eighth Dixie Walker doubled and Reese scored him with a single.

Dodger fans and the Dodgers themselves went home that night muttering about the tough break that knocked out Fitzsimmons when he was going so well. But this was nothing compared with the tough break Fate had prepared for the next day's game. It turned out to be a black day in Brooklyn's history, a game that has gone down as one of the most memorable in baseball legend. As broadcaster Red Barber often says, "It was something that could only have happened in Brooklyn."

Kirby Higbe started for the Dodgers, but got only as far as the fourth before the Yankees shelled him from the mound. They tapped him for one run in the first and two more in the fourth. Higbe stalked off to an early shower and French came in to relieve.

The Dodgers struck back in their half of the fourth. Owen and Coscarart walked. Wasdell batted for French and promptly banged a double off the right field wall that scored both runners. Then in the fifth Walker doubled, Reiser homered and the Dodgers took the lead, 4–3.

Hugh Casey, the crafty fireman, came in to protect the Dodgers' thin margin. He set the Yankees down without a murmur in the sixth, the seventh and the eighth. Came the ninth inning.

Dodger fans held their breaths as Casey got into the hole, three balls and one strike, on Yankee lead-off man, Johnny Sturm. A sharp curve made it three and two. Sturm swung on the next pitch and bounced to the right side. Coscarart glided over, gloved the ball and threw Sturm out by ten feet.

The dangerous Red Rolfe was next. Two outs to go— and the series all tied up. Rolfe bit at a change-up and dribbled the ball back to Casey. The pitcher looked at the ball for a minute, then hurled it to first. Two out. One more to go. A big one though—Tommy Henrich.

Casey worked carefully to "Old Reliable." And Henrich stood guarding the plate, working Casey to three and two, then fouling off a couple as the crowd became jittery with the tenseness of the moment. Casey peered down, took the sign from Owen. He wound up, then came down with a low, sweeping curve ball. Henrich swung— and missed! Strike three! The game was over!

But suddenly the crowd came to its feet and roared as the ball got through Owen and bounced off to the right of the plate. Henrich raced like a frightened jack rabbit down the line and beat Owen's frantic throw to first. He was safe! And the game wasn't over. The Yankees were still alive!

The Dodgers were stunned. The whole ball park was stunned. Instead of there being three out, there was Henrich perched on first base. It has been argued ever since that afternoon that someone on the Dodgers should have called time, in order to give Owen and Casey a chance to recover from the blow. But no one did. And the rest of the inning the Dodgers played like men in a trance.

DiMaggio stepped into the batter's box and Casey went right to work. DiMaggio singled to left. Up came Charlie Keller. Casey got two strikes on Keller; then, in his anxiety and shock, he tried to slip a third one past the Yankee slugger. Keller slammed it against the wall for a double. Both runners romped in and the Yankees led, 5–4.

Still, Dodger manager Durocher didn't stir from the bench. And no one on the field called for time out. Casey pitched now blindly, firing the ball at the plate in anger. He walked Dickey. Gordon doubled and Rizzuto walked. Johnny Murphy, the Yankees' reliever, bounced one into the hole between third and short. Reese sped over, reached across his body with his gloved hand, speared the ball and fired to first. The horror was over.

But the Yankees had scored four times, the Dodgers went out meekly in their half of the ninth and it was the Yankees' game, 7–4.

As far as everybody in baseball was concerned, the fifth game of the World Series was played just for the records. Nobody expected the Dodgers to come back after their heartbreaking luck of the past two days. Still, Whitlow Wyatt made a gallant effort the next day. But Ernie Bonham just toyed with the listless Dodger hitters and won it, 3–1. That was the World Series. About the only thing that could be said for it, in the Dodgers' behalf, was that but for two terrible breaks, the series might have gone the other way.

For Pee Wee Reese, even though he emerged as a full-fledged Dodger star, a World Series star, it was an empty, hollow triumph. For the beloved Bums had been thwarted by the Yankees, just when it seemed that victory was within their grasp.

CHAPTER 8

Amid the turmoil that followed in the wake of Pearl Harbor, little attention was paid by the newspapers or the Brooklyn Dodgers to their acquisition of utility out-fielder Johnny Rizzo. Johnny had knocked around the National League for years, playing unspectacularly with the Pirates, the Reds and the Phillies.

There was, in fact, little reason for anyone's noting Rizzo's arrival in the Dodger camp that spring of 1942. Not much was expected of him, and he was used sparingly during the season, winding up with a .220 batting average. To this very day few people know how much Johnny Rizzo contributed to the history of the Brooklyn Dodgers. And to one man's history in particular—that of Pee Wee Reese.

When Rizzo arrived in Havana, where the Dodgers were taking their spring training, the first thing that struck him was the "two weeks' vacation" air about the camp. The players were carrying on like a bunch of sales-men at a convention. The night spots and the movies were getting a big play from the Dodgers, and in the clubhouse every afternoon the only strategy the players had to worry about was the next night's movies or dinner party.

The laxness may have been partly due to the excitement and anxiety caused by the war. More likely, however, it was simply a case of the Dodgers becoming complacent and overconfident about their chances for the coming season.

"We're a cinch," one of the players confided to a newspaperman one night.

"Who's gonna beat us?" sneered another. "We'll win it by ten games at least."

The roistering among the Dodgers was pretty general, right up through the front office boss himself, Larry Mac-Phail. Though the Dodger executive expressed dislike with what he saw going on, he seemed to be in no position to stop it. When it came to such items as having a good time, or perhaps placing a few dollars on a horse, Mac-Phail was the first man to reach for his wallet.

There were a few notable exceptions on the team, however. Pee Wee Reese was one of them. The night clubs got no play from Pee Wee. Nor did the gambling dens. And it was not, as one writer jokingly put it, "With Reese's baby face, they wouldn't even let him in unless he was accompanied by an adult."

No, it was just that Pee Wee had more important things on his mind. He was far from sharing the overconfidence of his teammates—especially about his own playing. His happy World Series experience couldn't completely erase the memory of his terrible play during the regular 1941 season. He wasn't too worried about his hitting. That, he felt, would straighten out. It was his fielding that bothered him. It had always been his strong point. Now it was a glaring weak spot. Now he had a peculiar problem.

When Pee Wee came up to the Dodgers in 1940, his

fielding skill was unquestioned. Durocher marveled at the youngster's ball handling. "Of course," Leo told the baseball writers, "he couldn't carry my glove when I was in my prime. But did you ever see anybody go back after a pop fly like that little cockroach?"

And scout Ted McGrew told the writers, "In Louisville I watched that kid make some of the greatest plays I ever saw. I was scared out of my wits at the thought of losing him. Reese's great play in the slot was a thing worth seeing."

Even in 1941, when he played badly, "going into the slot" was a Pee Wee Reese specialty. It's about the toughest play for a shortstop to make. He has to go into the hole between shortstop and third base after a ground ball, and make an across the body stop with his gloved hand. He's then usually completely off balance for the long throw to first. Most good shortstops can field a ball hit into the slot; few can also throw out the runner afterward. Reese is one of those few.

Pee Wee's problem, then, was the long throw to first base, particularly after fielding a "ball in the slot." And the great majority of his errors the first two seasons with Brooklyn consisted of throwing errors.

And it was Leo Durocher's fault. Innocently, of course, but Leo Durocher's fault nonetheless. From the day Pee Wee reported to the Dodgers, Durocher tried to create a new Leo Durocher in Pee Wee Reese's image. Like father to son—and probably like Miller Huggins to Leo Durocher—that's the way Leo wanted it between himself and Pee Wee.

Reese did the best he could to live up to Leo's expectations. And by now he has more than fulfilled them. But at that point it only got him into trouble, because he had to change his fielding style trying to pattern himself after Durocher.

When he was playing Leo was one of the best there ever was at picking up a ground ball and flipping it to first in the same motion. He was a master at it. He tried to teach the movement to Reese, showed the youngster how to play in that fashion. As a result, Pee Wee found himself making the throw before he had the ball securely, or was out of position for a throw. Hence the many errors and wild throws.

This, then, was the problem Pee Wee wrestled with during the 1942 exhibition season. He knew it was something he had to lick—or his very baseball life was in danger. While his teammates cavorted in the Havana night clubs, Pee Wee lay awake in his room night after night, trying to figure a way out. In the afternoons, while the other players were relaxing in the sun, Pee Wee was out on the field practicing his throwing.

Johnny Rizzo found him at it one afternoon. The utility outfielder stood in front of the Dodger bench watching Pee Wee for a while, then walked out to the shortstop.

"You got your troubles, eh, Pee Wee?" he said in a friendly voice.

"Yeah, a little, Johnny," Reese admitted. "You notice anything peculiar about the way I field? You know, sometimes a guy who comes from another team has seen things a fellow's own teammates never notice."

Rizzo nodded. "I've been watching you. You got a name around the league as a hot shortstop. But you got a scatter arm. Hitters like to hit the ball your way. You might throw the ball into the grandstand. Then they get a base hit."

Pee Wee looked pained. "That's me all right. I think I know what's wrong, but I'd like to have somebody else see it and tell me. Do me a favor, will you, Johnny?" he said to Rizzo.

"Sure, Pee Wee."

"Watch me when we start playing the exhibition games. See if you can notice anything."

When the Dodgers moved their camp to Daytona, Florida, and started their spring exhibition series, Rizzo kept his eyes on Pee Wee. After a few games he reported to the Dodger shortstop.

"Your trouble, Pee Wee, is that you're trying to get the ball away too fast. You're throwing it even before you've got it. You're off balance. You're throwing before you're set to throw."

"I figured that's my trouble, too," said Pee Wee. "But what the heck should I do? When I wait till I field the ball cleanly before I throw, I waste too much time. That makes it easier for the runner to beat the throw. I just got to get the ball away fast as I can."

"That's because you're not throwing right," said Rizzo.

"What do you mean?" Reese asked, surprised.

"When you make your throws from a complete stop you throw overhand, right?"

Pee Wee thought a minute. "Yeah, picturing it in my mind, I guess that's right. So what?"

"So this. If you'd learn to throw kind of sidearm, or three quarters, you'd save that important split second it takes to crank your arm for the overhand throw. And in the second place, it's less wear and tear on your shoulders that way."

Reese appeared unconvinced.

"Get over at first base and throw me some grounders," Rizzo said. "I'll show you what I mean."

Reese's eyes opened wide as Rizzo demonstrated. First Johnny fielded a ground ball and threw to first with Reese's overhand motion. Then he threw with a sidearm motion, while his body was still in a crouch.

"Hey, maybe you got something there, Johnny!" Reese said. "I notice you don't have to straighten up to get your throw off, either. I can't throw overhand from a crouch."

"Right," said Rizzo. "Now I'll get over at first and throw some down to you and you can try it out. It'll take a little while for you to get comfortable, but once you do, I'm telling you, kid, it'll make a difference."

That might have been one of the prize baseball understatements of all time.

As the Dodgers' exhibition tour moved northward, the writers began to notice the change that had come over Pee Wee. His fielding was steadier; he moved with more assurance; there was less fumbling with ground balls.

The Dodgers, meanwhile, ebullient as ever, continued burning the midnight oil. Nobody, from bat boy to Larry MacPhail, recognized the handwriting on the wall.

Joe Medwick, knocked unconscious by a pitch the year before, was plate shy. Bush league pitchers the Dodgers were meeting in exhibition games got him out with ease. Camilli was sick on and off. Billy Herman was complaining that his left hip bothered him. Lavagetto had gone into service. But the Dodgers were walking around wearing their rose-colored glasses; they were cocky, still counting last year's World Series checks. And not a few were already counting the coming year's.

For awhile, indeed, their house of cards stood up, too. They jumped off to a good start, and by the middle of May they were six and a half games in front. The year before, when they won the pennant, their lead had never been more than four games.

And as always, in Brooklyn, life had its more humorous side. One day a man who lived near Ebbets Field got a court injunction to prevent Gladys Gooding, the Ebbets Field organist, from playing during the games. He claimed that the music disturbed his afternoon nap in his near-by apartment.

The complaint got little sympathy in a Brooklyn court. When the case was called the presiding magistrate looked down at the man angrily.

"What are you, a Giant fan?" he asked.

The injunction was withdrawn.

The Dodgers galloped on. They staved off a Cardinal surge in June. Everybody was hitting, and the pitchers were superb. They were still on top for the All-Star game break.

Pee Wee was riding high with the rest of the team, hitting well, fielding well. Sports writers talked of him as challenging Boston's Eddie Miller as king of the National League shortstops. With Miller, he was named to his first National League All-Star team.

In July a bean ball war started, with the rest of the league arrayed against the Dodgers. Everybody was out to get the Dodgers, it seemed. Their cockiness, their barbed bench jockeying and the brassy manner of Leo Durocher rankled opposing players to the point that when they played against Brooklyn, they played just a little bit harder and rougher.

The first casualty, however, had nothing to do with this war. But it turned out to be a tragic incident for the Dodgers, and even more for the player involved—Pete Reiser.

It happened on July 10th, a hot Sunday afternoon in St. Louis. It was the bottom of the twelfth inning, the score tied, two out for the Cardinals. Then Enos Slaughter hit a ball to the deepest part of center field. Reiser raced back and caught the ball on the dead run. But his next step sent him crashing into the bleacher wall. Slaughter sped around the bases for a home run that won the ball game.

Reiser was able to walk off the field, helped by his pal Reese, but he collapsed in the clubhouse. Rushed to a hospital, his injury was discovered to be a concussion of the brain. Although he was back in the line-up after a few days Reiser was never again the same ballplayer. Recurring headaches and muscular pains crippled him. He was hitting in the .350's when he crashed into the wall. The rest of the season he was a .220 hitter, winding up at .310.

In August the Dodgers still had a nine-game lead. And the smell of the World Series money was getting fresher in the players' nostrils every day. After one close game which the Dodgers won, Durocher clapped Larry MacPhail on the back. "What spirit this club's got. Everybody's happy."

"Yeah, that's the trouble," MacPhail growled. "Everybody's too happy. Nobody's worried. Nobody's hustling. You've got a fat, complacent ball club there, Leo. And I don't think you're going to win the pennant with them."

Durocher's mouth popped open. "You're crazy, Larry! We're ten games ahead of the Cardinals right now, and there's only a little over a month to go!"

"You should be twenty games in front!" snapped Mac-Phail. "And you would be if those guys would hustle. I'm warning you, Durocher, we're going to lose this pennant."

Durocher laughed. "Well, you're the only guy in baseball that thinks so."

If MacPhail was the only guy in baseball who thought so, then he was the only guy in baseball who was right. The Dodgers did not win the pennant.

In their behalf, though, it may be said that they didn't really lose it. During the month of September they won twenty and lost five, and also won their last eight games of the season. A pennant pace ordinarily, but the Cardinals caught fire in August and won thirty-seven of their last forty-three games. They won the pennant by two games.

In the gloomy aftermath of the season, there was at least one bright ray for the Dodgers. Pee Wee Reese had batted a fairly respectable .255. But he had led all the National League shortstops in double plays. The Dodgers were expecting a lot from Pee Wee during the next year.

Next year, however, Pee Wee was due to be wearing a **different uniform.**

CHAPTER 9

The Winter of 1942–43 saw the war make its first serious inroads into the structure of the major leagues. The armed services were reaching deeping and deeper into the barrel for man power; even men with dependents were being called up.

The Dodgers' Larry MacPhail was gone. The Dodger executive had tendered his resignation even before the 1942 season had ended. When the last game had been played, MacPhail made a speech of farewell and put on the uniform of a lieutenant colonel in the Army.

Larry French went into the Navy, together with Johnny Rizzo and Hugh Casey. Pete Reiser went into the Army. And on January 31, 1943, Pee Wee Reese enlisted in the Navy.

Until that time, Pee Wee had had a 3-A classification, with his mother and sister as dependents. In addition, he had married Dorothy Walton, she of the laughing eyes that had captivated Pee Wee in Louisville, the previous March. But in January the Army called him for re-examination and possible reclassification. Pee Wee decided to join the Navy.

As an apprentice seaman, Pee Wee reported to Commander Gene Tunney's school for physical education instructors at Norfolk, Virginia. After boot training and special schooling, Pee Wee was given a chief petty officer's rating. He stayed a year at Norfolk, playing on the base nine along with teammate Hugh Casey.

In January, 1944, Pee Wee got his orders to ship out to the Pacific. He was ordered to report to Lieutenant-Commander Edwin Haislet in Hawaii. The day his ship sailed for Honolulu, his daughter Barbara was just two weeks old.

Hugh Casey shipped out with Pee Wee and for a while they played against each other in Hawaii, until Pee Wee left for a tour of the Pacific. Judging from Reese's experiences with Casey, the Dodger pitcher must have livened up the Pacific almost as much as the Japanese.

The first time Pee Wee batted against the old fireball, Casey threw a fast ball that sailed right behind Reese's head. Pee Wee hit the ground in a cloud of dust, his bat flying out of his hand. He got up, dusted himself off and looked out at the mound. Casey was grinning from ear to ear.

On the next pitch Pee Wee lashed a line drive right back through the pitcher's legs. Casey had to scramble like a rabbit to keep from having his feet fly out from under him. As Reese took his lead off first base, Casey looked over at him. Now Pee Wee was grinning from ear to ear.

Next time up Pee Wee hit the deck again as Casey turned his cap around with a fast ball. But when the game was over the pitcher came over to Pee Wee and clapped him on the back.

"What's the matter, kid?" he said. "You ain't looking so good."

"How would you look with a ball stuck in your ear?"

Reese answered with a grin. "You ought to be ashamed of yourself, Casey. Don't you remember me—Pee Wee, your old teammate?"

"Gee, I'm sorry, Pee Wee," Casey said, with mock seriousness. "But the darned ball kept slipping."

"Yeah, I guess it did," said Pee Wee. "If your control was any better you wouldn't have missed."

"Aw, now, Pee Wee," the pitcher protested.

"Hughie," Reese laughed, shaking his head, "you're a great guy. Off the field, though. I'll bet in a ball game you'd even throw at your own mother."

Casey seemed to think for a minute. "Well," he said firmly, "only if she was crowding the plate."

That fall, Reese playing in the service "world series," found himself sandwiched between two Yankees. Phil Rizzuto played third and Joe Gordon held down second.

From the newspapers sent to him regularly, Pee Wee followed the fortunes of the Dodgers. Branch Rickey was now general manager of the Brooklyn club. With Larry MacPhail gone, the board of directors decided to bring a new kind of management to Brooklyn. MacPhail was the bright lights lover, the horse player; Rickey was a quiet homebody. He neither drank nor gambled, and had never condoned either on any ball club he'd ever run. He was just the man, it was felt, to end the Dodgers' carousing and the parade of bookies in the clubhouse.

In 1943, Pee Wee read with disappointment of the Dodgers' third-place finish. In 1944, he followed their misfortunes with horror as the patchwork team finished a dismal seventh. In 1945, however, the Dodgers bounced back to third place.

But Pee Wee's most significant bit of reading came in

the winter of 1945. After a tour of Pacific bases, Pee Wee was being shipped back to the States for discharge.

He was sitting on deck of the ship that was carrying him from Guam, when a shipmate walked over to him with a tattered copy of a United States newspaper.

"Hey, Pee Wee," said the sailor, "take a look at what it says here in the paper about the Dodgers."

Pee Wee glanced at the headline in the newspaper. "It says 'Dodgers sign Jackie Robinson.' So? Who's he? I don't remember seeing his name around before."

"Man, you're getting fat and lazy sitting around on deck," the sailor said, snatching back the paper. "Here, I'll read what it says. 'The Brooklyn Dodgers yesterday announced the signing of infielder Jackie Robinson to a contract for an undisclosed amount. Robinson is expected to play with the Dodgers' farm club at Montreal next season. He is the first Negro to be admitted to the ranks of organized baseball.' "

The sailor thrust the newspaper at Reese. "Here, read it yourself, man. Read how you're going to play alongside of a colored boy."

"What for?" Reese responded. "You just read it to me."

"Is that all you got to say?" the sailor demanded. "This Robinson's a Negro! What are you going to do about that!"

Pee Wee, Kentucky born and bred, looked up at his shipmate calmly. "Does it say what position the guy plays?"

"Shortstop," the sailor said impatiently.

Pee Wee sighed. "How do you like that. Another guy I'll have to beat out for a job."

* * *

Pee Wee Reese walked up the steps of the dugout and stepped out onto the playing field, blinking at the brightness of the Florida sun after the darkness of the locker room.

"Well, look who's here," a voice came to him. "The pride of the Navy. How're you, Pee Wee?"

Reese turned around. "Hi, Hig, how's it going?" he said to Kirby Higbe, shaking the pitcher's hand warmly.

A hand tapped Pee Wee on the shoulder. "Hey, son, tryout camp is over. Why don't you come back next year?"

"Casey, you old son of a gun! It's good to see you again," said Pee Wee whirling to greet the speaker.

Hugh Casey looked Pee Wee up and down. "Why, it's Pee Wee Reese himself," he said feigning surprise. "I didn't recognize you for a minute. I thought you were one of them kids down here to try out." He looked at Reese again appraisingly. "You put on a few pounds, kid, but you still look like you ain't dry behind the ears yet."

Pee Wee grinned. "I'm lucky I've got ears at all after batting against you in Hawaii," he said.

"Gee, look at the paunch on him, will you, Hughie?" Higbe said to Hugh Casey. "He'll soon look like Ted McGrew if he's not careful," Higbe said, referring to the rotund scout.

"Yeah, we'll have to watch this guy at the table," agreed Casey with mock seriousness. "He was one of the biggest chow hounds in the Navy. I'll bet they discharged him because they couldn't afford to feed him anymore."

"You guys laugh all you want," Pee Wee grinned. "But I'm feeling great." He patted his stomach. "I only weigh one hundred seventy-two, about fifteen pounds more than when I went in."

"Don't worry, we'll take that lard off you," growled Leo Durocher, walking up to the three players. He stuck out his hand. "Whatta you say, Pee Wee, how they treat you in the Navy?"

"Can't kick, Leo. I had it a lot better than most guys."

"Yeah, I'm sure sorry I missed out on going in," Durocher shook his head. "But this ear of mine!" The Army had rejected Durocher for a punctured eardrum. "Well, take things easy for a couple of days, Pee Wee," he said. "You know, run around, get loosened up a little."

Pee Wee nodded agreement.

"You play much ball in the Navy?" the Dodger manager asked.

"Yes, plenty of it."

"Good. That'll help. We're really counting on you this year, you know," Durocher said. Then he slapped Pee Wee on the back. "Awful glad to see you back, son. Sure missed having you around. Now let's get to work. Counting an awful lot on you this year, Pee Wee."

Two weeks later Pee Wee was the talk of the Dodger camp. His teammates and the writers covering the Dodgers were high in their praise of the Dodgers' shortstop.

"Reese is one of the greatest shortstops baseball has ever seen," Hugh Casey told one of the writers. "He's improved one hundred per cent over the player he was before he was in the Navy."

"Watching him out there, day after day, playing himself into shape, the impression grows that Reese can be the best shortstop in baseball this season," wrote Frank Graham of the New York *Journal-American*. "All his old speed and bounce is there, plus the assurance and poise that comes with added years."

Leo Durocher was the most enthusiastic of all. "I wouldn't trade Reese for Marty Marion or anybody else," said Durocher in answer to a question by Eddie Murphy of the New York *Sun*. The St. Louis Cardinal player then had the reputation of being one of baseball's greatest shortstops.

"Reese is the best shortstop in the National League, bar none," Durocher continued.

"Do you think Pee Wee Reese is a better shortstop than a fellow named Leo Durocher was when he was playing ball?" asked Murphy.

"Yes, I do," Durocher answered unhesitatingly. "They tell me I was pretty good as a shortstop, but in my opinion Pee Wee is a marvel."

"At what do you figure Reese is better than you were?"

"Just about everything," Leo snapped.

"Coming from Durocher," Murphy commented the next day, "that was quite an admission."

Pee Wee, however, was making all his supporters look good. His extra weight turned into muscle; he set about busting the fences up and down the grapefruit circuit, as the players called the exhibition game tours.

After one such game, in which Pee Wee racked up two doubles and a single as the Dodgers beat the Yankees, 10–6, Bill Dickey added his praise to the collection.

"Reese was the best ballplayer I saw in the Pacific," said the veteran Yankee catcher. "And it looks like he's going to be just about the best shortstop around the major leagues, too."

There was plenty of other excitement around the

Dodger camp that spring of 1946. Jorge Pasquel, a Mexican with big ideas and a bank roll to match, started to make a grab at American ballplayers for his new Mexican League. Waving a reported forty thousand dollar contract at Luis Olmo, he made the Dodger outfielder his first catch on the Dodgers. Next went catcher Mickey Owen. There wasn't much Branch Rickey could do about Pasquel, but when the brassy Mexican sent an agent right into the Dodger camp at Daytona Beach, the Dodger general manager lost his temper.

Rickey caught the agent, one Señor Jaimes, right in the act of offering one of the Dodgers a contract. He chased the agent clear out of the ball park, puffing on his ever-present cigar all the while. "I'm an old man!" Rickey yelled through his clenched teeth. "But I'll beat your head in if you bother my players again!" Pee Wee Reese listened to the players talking about the big money in the Mexican League, but he turned a deaf ear to all of Pasquel's offers. He was happy with his spot with the Dodgers.

With Pee Wee Reese blasting the way with a spring average of .414, the Dodgers came into the regular season under a full head of steam. It was the year of Rickey's "Youth Movement." The outfield had all rookies—Dick Whitman, Carl Furillo and Gene Hermanski. The catcher was a rookie, too, Ferrell Anderson. Except for veteran Billie Herman at third base, the infield, though experienced, was a young one. Reese was at short, Eddie Stanky at second and Eddie Stevens at first.

The Dodgers won eight and lost three in April. But so did the Cardinals, a sign of things to come that year. Then they won nine straight at Ebbets Field, but flopped on the road. One day they led the league; the next day the Cardinals were on top.

And on May 23, Pee Wee Reese officially became a Dodger. He got into a fight.

The day before there had been a brawl on the field when Lennie Merullo, Chicago Cub shortstop, and Eddie Stanky got into a rhubarb. Merullo later claimed somebody hit him from behind as the players broke up the fight.

The next afternoon Pee Wee Reese was in the batting cage, taking his practice swings, when Merullo approached him menacingly.

"They tell me you were the guy who slugged me yesterday when I was fighting Stanky," said Merullo. "I never saw your face. I'd like to fight you when I can see it, and I can see it now."

With that Merullo cocked his fist and moved in on Reese. Pee Wee set himself, ready for Merullo. But Dixie Walker, who had been standing near by, jumped on the wild-eyed Cub and dragged him away. Merullo threw a punch at Walker, then a wild melee took place as both teams poured into the fray.

Phil Cavaretta squared off against Reese, but found himself in the clutches of Anderson, the Dodgers' huge catcher. All through the fight, Anderson carried the Cubs' little outfielder Peanuts Lowery around on his back like a jockey. Lowery kept pounding away at the big catcher, but Anderson just ignored him.

When the Ebbets Field police, aided by a squad of the regular police, finally broke it up, Walker was found to be the only player seriously damaged. His face was cut and he was minus a tooth.

The Ebbets Field crowd buzzed for the rest of the afternoon, hoping for a new outbreak, but three policemen in each dugout kept things quiet. Not so quiet, however, that umpire Jocko Conlan didn't have to throw Leo Durocher out of the game in the ninth inning.

According to observers, the Dodgers appeared to have lost the pregame fight. But they won the day's game—a thriller, too. And Pee Wee got back at the Cubs in the most effective way, by driving in the winning run in the eleventh inning.

Toward the end of June, Bruce Edwards was brought up from Mobile, Joe Medwick was brought back from retirement—to fill in as a pinch hitter—and the Dodgers jumped out to a seven-game lead over the Cardinals.

Four Dodgers were named for the All-Star game, to be played on July 9th—Walker, Reese, Reiser and Higbe. But the Cardinals, as an indication of the power they were soon to show, placed six men on the team—outfielders Enos Slaughter and Stan Musial, third baseman Whitey Kurowski, shortstop Marty Marion, second baseman Red Schoendienst and Pitcher Howie Pollet.

Pee Wee, however, missed the All-Star game. A chipped vertebra in his neck not only made him miss the classic, but sidelined him for ten days. By the time he got back into the line-up, the Cardinals were breathing right down the Dodgers' necks.

For the rest of the season, the pendulum swung back and forth. First the Cardinals were on a streak, then the Dodgers. The lead changed hands constantly. It was thrilling baseball, one of the greatest pennant fights in years, and the crowds that flocked to Ebbets Field proved it.

They can't make finishes any closer than the one between the Dodgers and the Cardinals in 1946. The race ended in a tie.

The Dodgers, however, couldn't do a thing right in the play-off series that followed. The Cardinals took two straight, 4–2, and 8–4, and that was the pennant.

It was Pee Wee's greatest year. He emerged as a full-fledged star. He led the National League again in double plays for a shortstop, batted .284, hit ten triples and batted in sixty runs.

At the season's end, Milt Gross, writing under his column in the New York *Post,* said of Pee Wee: "Reese entered the Navy in 1943 as a brilliant, but scatter-armed shortstop. He came out ten or fifteen pounds heavier and also as the best shortstop in the National League . . . he was the Dodgers' most consistent performer of the season."

So the Brooklyn players scattered for their winter of fishing, or selling cars or loafing, while Dodger fans muttered their famous slogan, "Wait till next year!"

Wait till next year, indeed. What a season that was going to be!

CHAPTER **10**

Ask most anybody connected with major league baseball, "What kind of guy is Pee Wee Reese?" and they'll probably give you the same answer: "You want to know what kind of guy Pee Wee is? Ask Jackie Robinson."

As a veteran of eight seasons with the Dodgers, Jackie Robinson is well qualified to pass an opinion on his teammate. As the first Negro to play in organized baseball, Robinson is probably better qualified to comment on Pee Wee Reese than anybody else in the game.

Robinson's eyes glow with respect and admiration when he talks of Pee Wee. "I'll talk about Reese any hour of any day," Robinson says. "Everybody respects and loves that fellow. In my book there's none finer than Pee Wee Reese. A real nice man is a rare thing. The crowd always spots him. And they sure guessed right about Pee Wee. I could tell you plenty."

Robinson could tell, for example, about his first year with the Dodgers in 1947, and the maneuverings of Branch Rickey to ease his path to the major leagues. The Dodgers' general manager never underestimated the enormity of the project of having a Negro accepted in baseball. There was no doubt about Robinson's qualifications after his sensational season at Montreal the year before. But Rickey wanted the Dodger players to accept

Robinson, want him as an asset to the club, rather than force them to play alongside of him.

To that end Rickey had the Dodgers train in Havana that spring, and scheduled exhibition games with Cuban and South American teams. This would afford the Dodger players an opportunity to become accustomed to playing baseball with Negroes, and would avoid the segregation problems that would have cropped up in Florida.

Until the last minute, Robinson was kept with the Montreal squad. Rickey felt that it would be wise to let the Dodgers meet Robinson, and get to know him, without the prior knowledge that he was definitely going to be brought up that year. As the players showed signs of accepting Robinson, the strategy was to have Leo Durocher pop off to the sports writers that he wanted Rickey to bring Robinson up, that the Dodgers needed him. Unfortunately, Durocher wasn't around to make the speech.

On the day the "ad lib" statement was to be made to the reporters, Durocher was informed that he was suspended from baseball for a year. This was the result of an accumulation of troubles with the baseball commissioner's office about Leo's off-the-field associations with questionable persons, and the aftermath of a squabble in Havana with the Yankees over the presence of gamblers at an exhibition game between the two clubs.

A few days later, the Dodgers quietly announced that they had purchased the contract of Jackie Robinson from the Montreal club.

The tremendous pressure on Robinson all this time was generally understood. But what was less generally realized was the pressure on the Dodger players, particularly those players from the South, who had definite convictions about the status of Negroes. Most of these, as they got to know Robinson, changed their minds, or at least accepted him. Only one Dodger asked to be traded—and was, the following year.

Pee Wee Reese, for one, gave the problem a lot of thought. Before he had reported to Havana that spring, his neighbors in Louisville had put him through the wringer on the subject of Robinson.

"What about Robinson?" they would ask Reese, stopping him on the street, "You going to play ball with a Negro? You going to room with him? You going to eat and sleep in the same hotel with a Negro?"

Pee Wee lay awake many nights thinking of the answers to questions like these, and questions that formed in his own mind. Even Pee Wee's family, Kentuckians for many generations, asked him about Robinson.

Just before he left home for spring training, his wife Dorothy asked him, "What will you do if they want Robinson to play with the Dodgers this season, Harold?"

"What do you think I should do?" Pee Wee asked.

"Whatever you think is the right thing. And whatever you really feel."

"I'll tell you, honey," Pee Wee said slowly. "Sit down a minute," he said indicating a chair in their living room. "I've been lying awake night after night thinking about this thing. It's really a tough problem, not an easy thing to work out."

"I understand," his wife said.

"You know how it is, honey. I've been thinking about what our friends would say, our families and all. Everybody around here keeps asking me, 'What about Robinson? What about Robinson?' To tell the truth, honey, I just don't know what about Robinson."

Pee Wee's wife nodded understandingly. "It's not something you can just decide overnight, Harold. But do you know anything about Robinson? I mean, what kind of man is he? You know what I mean."

"I never met the guy," Pee Wee said. "But, well here's the way I feel about him now. I know Rickey—and if he signed Robinson, then he must be good enough to play for the Dodgers. And again, if I know Rickey, Robinson must be a pretty good guy."

"That's true," Dorothy admitted.

"So it's this way, honey. I've been thinking, if this Robinson is a good enough player to help the team, and if he's a nice guy, well . . . why should his being on the team bother me?"

"You mean, then," his wife said, "that you wouldn't mind if Robinson played?"

"Under those circumstances, I guess I'd have to say that's right. At least I don't feel I won't want him under any conditions. It'll really have to wait, I guess, until I get to know the guy."

"All right, dear," Dorothy said. "I think it's a good thing we had this talk, and that I know how you feel. Because if Robinson does play, I'm going to be getting plenty of questions around here myself. And I want to be able to answer them honestly. And I want you to know, too, that I'm right at your side in any arguments about this thing."

Pee Wee got up and kissed his wife affectionately. "Thanks, hon. Don't think knowing that won't help. It means a lot to me. What's more, I kind of feel that since

I wore the uniform of the United States Navy and tried to do my bit in the war against the Nazis, I want to feel that a guy like Robinson or any guy, regardless of race or creed, ought to have a chance to play baseball with the Dodgers or any club he wants to. That's the way I feel about it!"

It didn't take Pee Wee very long to make up his mind about Robinson. After the first couple of weeks of spring training Reese said to one of the writers traveling with the Dodgers, "You know, my first feelings about Robinson were that, after all, maybe he's just as good as I am. Now, after meeting him and seeing what kind of wonderful guy he is, I've reached the conclusion that maybe he's a better man than I am."

Once having made up his mind about Jackie, Pee Wee decided it was necessary to do more than just passively accept Robinson's presence on the team. He would go out of his way to make a place for Jackie, to show him that he was acknowledged as a man and a player, the same as any other member of the Dodgers. Pee Wee soon found ample opportunity to show Robinson how things stood between them.

When the Dodgers checked in at Macon, Georgia, for a preseason exhibition game, Robinson received a letter warning him that he would be shot if he appeared on the field that day.

As the Dodgers warmed up on the sidelines before the day's game, Reese noticed that Robinson was standing near by, throwing the ball back and forth with another teammate.

"Hey, get away from me, you human target," Pee Wee called to Robinson. "With my luck that guy'll take a shot at you and hit me by mistake. And I don't look good with holes in me." The Dodger players around the pair burst out laughing, and Robinson grinned at Pee Wee's ribbing.

"I had been tied up in scared little knots," Robinson said after the game. "But when Pee Wee started kidding me, everything kind of loosened up inside me. I didn't feel so alone any more. I felt that at last I finally was a member of the ball club."

That's the way it went all season long. During infield practice before each game, Pee Wee made it a point to stand around and chat with Robinson. During the game itself, he would call time every once in a while and confer with the infielders at the pitcher's mound, just so he could talk again with Robinson. Then, as they trotted back to their positions, Pee Wee always remembered to give Jackie a friendly pat on the back.

All this had a deep effect on the fans and the players. As one member of another team put it, "Most of us weren't in favor of Robinson playing against us, and we rode him pretty hard—and rough. But everybody in this league's got a lot of respect for Reese. And when we'd see him out there, talking and laughing with Robinson like they were the best of buddies, we began to figure, well, maybe Robinson isn't too bad a guy after all."

One time in Philadelphia, a fan sitting right behind the Dodger dugout began shouting insults at Jackie. Everybody in the park could hear the man's voice. Robinson, on the field, just bit his lip and made believe he heard nothing. Suddenly Pee Wee called time, walked over to Robinson, put his arm around his neck and started talking.

It quieted Robinson's jangling nerves, but it couldn't quiet the fan. He switched his insults to Pee Wee. Reese grinned and shouted across the diamond to Robinson, "How do you like that guy? I take him off your back and he gets on mine."

There was more to it, however, than just backing up Robinson on the field. On the Dodgers' first road trip in 1947, Reese and catcher Bruce Edwards took advantage of an open afternoon to play golf. Halfway through their game, they saw Robinson behind them, playing alone.

"Hey, Jackie," Pee Wee called out. "Don't be so darned exclusive. Come on over and join us."

When the 1947 season was over, and Robinson was handed the Rookie of the Year award, he gave all the credit to Reese. "Pee Wee did so many things to help me," Jackie said. "So many for which I'll be eternally grateful to him."

When Reese was told of Robinson's words, he smiled. "I'll tell you this," Pee Wee said, "nobody in baseball ever had a tougher job breaking in than Robinson. I realized that when I tried to put myself in his shoes. What pressure was on that guy! Everybody was watching him, writing about him. But nobody wanted him. If he failed to make the grade, the colored race would probably never get another chance at major league baseball. And the other teams took advantage of all that. The pitchers put a little extra on the ball against Jackie, and they dusted him off plenty. The infielders and outfielders tried just a little harder to get him out.

"I asked myself how I would do under those circumstances. And to tell you the truth I didn't come out too well. I don't think I could have made it. And certainly not the way Jackie did. Did I help him? If I helped Jackie Robinson," Pee Wee said, "it was as much to win back my self-respect as anything else."

CHAPTER 11

The news that Leo Durocher was suspended for the 1947 season hit the baseball world like a bombshell. Leo "The Lip" was not exactly held in fond esteem by the opposition, but even his bitterest enemies could find no precedent for such action based on the vague charge of "conduct detrimental to baseball."

Durocher was out as manager of the Dodgers, nevertheless. It remained, then, for Branch Rickey to come up with a successor to pilot the Dodgers for the coming season.

Rickey called a staff meeting at the Dodgers' Montague Street offices in Brooklyn, and went down the list of possible candidates. There was Clay Hopper, manager of the Montreal club, and Burt Shotton, who was looking after some Dodger youngsters down around Miami and Cuba.

"How about Joe McCarthy?" someone suggested. "Especially after quitting MacPhail and the Yankees, he might go for the idea of coming over with us."

Joe McCarthy was called, but declined the offer.

"Bill McKechnie," said another member of the Dodgers' staff. "He's doing a good job coaching with Cleveland."

"How about Bill Terry?"

"Why don't we try Rogers Hornsby, Branch?"

One of the Dodger coaches cleared his throat. "It's occurred to me, Mr. Rickey, that while we're trying to find a new manager, we ought to get someone to direct the team on the field at least. We open in a few days, you know."

"You have anybody in particular in mind?" Rickey asked.

"Pee Wee Reese."

Rickey's shaggy eyebrows shot up. "A very interesting recommendation. Very interesting, indeed." The Dodger executive tilted his chair back and looked at the ceiling, sending billowing plumes of cigar smoke upward, as if deliberately to symbolize that the intricate machinery of his mind was hard at work.

Suddenly he sent his chair tilting forward again and leaned across his desk. "Yes, an interesting suggestion by all means. But not yet. Yes, someday we must see to it. But not yet."

He sent his chair swiveling sideward. "How about you, Clyde?" he said to coach Clyde Sukeforth. "I think you can run the team on the field until we get someone to steer this ship of ours."

"I don't know, B. R.," the coach hesitated. "I'd like to give it a little thought."

"We don't have any more time for thought," Rickey thundered. "In the absence of any qualified volunteers for the job, it behooves you to take it on."

"All right," Sukeforth sighed. "You talked me into it."

Rickey slammed his palm on the desk. "Good! Now, gentlemen, let us see to our opening day line-up."

Though the Dodgers appeared on opening day without a definite manager, they nevertheless fielded a pennant potential line-up. With the sterling double-play combination of Reese and Stanky on hand, Rickey had converted Jackie Robinson to a first baseman. Jackie was no Sisler around the bag, but he'd more than do. At third was young Johnny Jorgensen, with Cookie Lavagetto to alternate.

The Dodgers had four top-flight outfielders—Dixie Walker, Pete Reiser, Gene Hermanski and Carl Furillo. Catching was Bruce Edwards. The pitching staff was good as well as deep, with Ralph Branca, Hank Behrman, Vic Lombardi, Harry Taylor, Joe Hatten, Rex Barney and the old reliable of the bull pen, Hugh Casey.

Under Sukeforth's handling, the Dodgers won their first two games of the season. Rickey appeared content to go on that way, but the Dodger coaches banded together and appealed to Rickey to bring Burt Shotton up to manage the club.

Under the sixty-three-year-old Shotton, who had been in semi-retirement for a number of years, the Dodgers won eight of their first ten. The Dodgers were riding high.

They were promptly brought to earth, however, by their first western trip. They lost eleven and won only six on that disastrous swing, and when they came dragging back to Brooklyn, they were in fifth place.

Still, the Dodgers were really too good a ball club to keep down. They got hot again, went on a winning streak and threatened for the league lead. The pitching staff righted itself and the hitters started showing their muscles.

Strangely enough, the Dodgers' strongest show of muscle was coming from a least expected quarter—Pee Wee Reese. In his first four years with Brooklyn, Pee Wee hit a total of fifteen home runs. Now, suddenly he seemed to have become the poor man's Babe Ruth.

He hit twelve home runs in 1947—no threat to the Bambino's record, to be sure, but a considerable number in view of the total of his four previous seasons. What's more, Pee Wee had his first ten round trippers in by July 4th, and one of them was a grand slam homer that beat the Pirates on June 4th.

"I don't know what it is," Pee Wee grinned, when a writer asked him about his sudden show of power. "I'm swinging the way I always have. The ball just seems to be going into the stands. If anybody sees anything different, I wish he'd tell me. I'd sure like to keep it up."

Nobody spotted the secret, if there was one, and the home run epidemic stopped. Fortunately, however, Pee Wee's timely hitting did not. In July, with the Dodgers leading the league but threatened by a resurgent Cardinal team, they came into St. Louis for an important three-game series.

Harry Taylor shut out the Cardinals in the first game. And Ralph Branca was coasting along with a 10–0 lead in the second game, until the roof fell in. Branca was suddenly shelled off the mound. The usually competent Hugh Casey was likewise blasted to the showers. In the ninth inning the Cardinals tied the score and had the winning run on third when Clyde King finally put out the fire.

Two innings later, with two out and Bruce Edwards on second, Pee Wee singled to right center, scoring Edwards with the winning run.

Pee Wee won another game the very next day. This time it was little Vic Lombardi's game Pee Wee saved. In the eighth inning, with the score tied, Dodgers on first and second, Pee Wee was flashed the hit-and-run sign. As Cardinal hurler Howie Pollet came down with his pitch, Pee Wee shifted his feet slightly and drove as neat a hit down the right field line as anyone would want to see on a hit-and-run play. Both runners, off and running with the pitch, scampered around and scored as Reese pulled into second. That took care of the ball game.

But against the Chicago Cubs one afternoon at Ebbets Field, Pee Wee was involved in the most embarrassing incident of his baseball life. He was on first with a walk, and Dixie Walker was the man at the plate.

Johnny Schmitz, the Cub pitcher, was a top hand with a change-up curve. With the count one ball and one strike on Walker, he got the Dodger outfielder to go fishing for one of his change-up specialties. The bat slipped out of Walker's hands, as he missed the pitch, and went sailing over toward first base. Pee Wee, his mind apparently somewhere else, walked off first, picked up the bat and started to flip it back to Walker.

The Cub catcher, Clyde McCullough, was so startled to see Reese calmly walk off base that he almost forgot to throw. But then he snapped the ball down to Eddie Waitkus at first, and Reese was out by a mile.

The next morning, Pee Wee got a telegram from Leo Durocher, who was following the Dodgers from his exile in California. The message was brief: "Next time don't be such a nice guy."

The Dodgers rode a handy lead through most of the summer. The Cardinals repeatedly made threatening gestures, but couldn't catch up. Late in August the Reds came into Ebbets Field for four games.

Ewell Blackwell, the right-hander with the sidearm delivery that dubbed him "the whip," opened against the Dodgers. With Pete Reiser on third in the late innings, the Reds' catcher let a pitch get away. Reiser charged down the line and Blackwell came in to cover the plate.

Hugh Poland, the catcher, recovered the ball, but threw high to Blackwell. The pitcher stretched for the throw. Reiser, barreling in, hit him, and Blackwell folded like an empty sack.

The Reds hollered foul and threatened to get even. And the next day they did. Reese, beating out a bunt, had his foot stepped on by first baseman Bert Haas. The spikes severed an artery in Pee Wee's foot and he hobbled around on crutches for a week.

With all their troubles, the Dodgers managed to stagger in to the pennant, five games ahead of the St. Louis Cardinals.

Two Dodgers, Bruce Edwards and Jackie Robinson, were among the first five in the voting for the Most Valuable Player award that year, won by Bob Elliott of the Braves. But when all the statistics were in, Pee Wee Reese was the man who got on base more times than any other Dodger. He also tied with Hank Greenberg of the Pirates for the most bases on balls received—one hundred four. For the third straight year he led the National League shortstops in double plays, and he had been named to the All-Star team.

For the second year in a row, Pee Wee hit .284. He hit twelve home runs, twenty-four doubles and batted in seventy-three runs. He had quite a year for himself.

He was to have quite a World Series, too.

CHAPTER 12

The 1947 Dodgers earned the distinction of carrying the Yankees to seven games in the series, something previous National League clubs had found almost impossible to do. But they still came out on the short end of the series fight.

The Yankees had most of their players from their championship clubs of 1942 and 1943 still active—men like Joe DiMaggio, Tommy Henrich, Charlie Keller, Johnny Lindell, Phil Rizzuto, Billy Johnson and Spud Chandler.

To this powerful array they had added Snuffy Stirnweiss at second, George McQuinn at first, Yogi Berra behind the plate and pitchers Allie Reynolds, Vic Raschi, Frank Shea, Floyd Bevans, Bobo Newsom, Carl Drews and relief specialist Joe Page.

The Yankee Stadium attendance for the first game of the series—73,365—broke all records. But this was little solace for the Dodger fans among the crowd.

Ralph Branca, the Dodgers' twenty-one-game winner, started against Frank Shea. For the first four innings the Yankees couldn't touch Branca, twelve men in a row going down before the young right-hander. The Dodgers, meanwhile, nicked Shea for a run in the first inning.

Joe DiMaggio started things for the Yankees in the fifth with a single to deep short that Reese made a great stop on, but couldn't throw. Branca walked McQuinn and hit Johnson with a pitch, filling the bases with nobody out. Lindell doubled in two runs and Rizzuto walked, filling the bases again. Branca went two balls and no strikes on Bobby Brown, then was replaced by Hank Behrman.

Behrman finished the walk to Brown, forcing in the third Yankee run. Stirnweiss hit a wicked liner to short that Reese knocked down and threw home for the force out. Henrich singled for two more runs, but Berra popped to third to end the bombardment. Five runs were across, proving to be all the Yankees needed.

The Dodgers shelled Joe Page, who relieved Shea, in the sixth and seventh, but couldn't break through, scoring single tallies in each inning. Final score: Yankees 5, Dodgers 3.

In the second game, the Yankees combed four Brooklyn hurlers for fifteen hits and an easy 10–3 victory. Vic Lombardi, Hal Gregg, Hank Behrman and Rex Barney were the victims of the Yankee power, and the papers started talking about another Yankee four-straight blitzkrieg.

But the Dodgers were a long way from being dead. Back on their home grounds for the third game of the series, they went to work on their ex-teammate Bobo Newsom. With one out in the second inning, Hermanski walked and Edwards doubled him home. Pee Wee Reese singled, scoring Edwards. Jorgensen went out, but pitcher Hatten singled, Stanky doubled Reese in for the third run and Hatten scored on a passed ball by Sherman Lollar.

The portly Newsom trudged off the mound and handed the ball to Vic Raschi. Robinson singled and Furillo doubled for the fifth and sixth runs before Walker was retired to close out the inning.

The Yankees kept chipping away at the Dodgers' lead, but the Brooks added a run in the third and two more in the fourth. When Yogi Berra's pinch hit home run off Branca in the seventh made the Dodger lead a slim one run, 9–8, Shotton called in Hugh Casey.

With an assist by Reese, Casey nailed down the victory. In the eighth inning, Henrich opened by working the Dodger reliefer for a pass. When Lindell followed with a single and Joe DiMaggio walked up to the plate, the Dodger bull pen swung furiously into action.

Casey went to two balls and one strike on Joe. Then he tried to slip a change-up past DiMag. Joe timed the pitch neatly and cracked it right past Casey's legs. The ball kicked up a little cloud of dust as it hit behind the mound like a rifleshot, then skimmed out toward center field.

Reese took off like a frightened rabbit when he saw the ball hit and, with a frantic dive, gloved it deep behind second. The ball was hit so sharply that Stanky hadn't had time to get over to second, but Pee Wee flipped a beautiful toss toward the bag. The ball and Stanky got to second together, and the little second baseman fired to first to double up DiMaggio.

Ebbets Field was a madhouse. Instead of it being tie score, nobody out and two Yankees on base, there were two out, one runner on, and the Dodgers still had their lead. Casey, given a tremendous lift by Reese's great play, retired McQuinn easily and set the Yankees down in order in the ninth.

The fourth game of the 1947 World Series is now legend in baseball. It combined heartbreak and heroics, real drama that had baseball fans talking about nothing else for weeks afterward.

Dodger manager Burt Shotton took a chance on starting Harry Taylor, though the sore-armed pitcher hadn't toiled for a month and a half. Stirnweiss greeted Taylor with a single. Henrich did the same. Berra exploded a line drive right at Reese's feet. Pee Wee stayed with the ball, but it crawled up his arm and bounced away. It was scored an error and the bases were loaded.

Coach Clyde Sukeforth called time and strode out to the mound. "I guess this isn't your day, Harry. Maybe you'd better sit the rest of the game out."

"But I've been saving my arm," protested Taylor. "I haven't even started to throw hard yet, Sukey."

"When do you figure on starting?" growled the coach, looking around at the loaded bases. "There's no place left to put anybody."

"Don't worry, Sukey. They won't get another hit off me this inning."

Sukeforth went back to the bench, but made sure that the Dodger bull pen got to work.

Joe DiMaggio stepped into the batter's box—and Taylor was right. Not another Yankee got a hit off him that inning. He walked DiMaggio to force a run across and Hal Gregg was waved in to take over.

Pee Wee, fretting at shortstop over his error, soon had the chance to more than make up for it.

McQuinn, first man up against Gregg, hit a little looper into left that had "Texas League single" written all over it. But this kind of thing was Pee Wee's specialty. He turned his back to the plate, raced back and took the fading ball over his shoulder on the dead run. He was keeping the Dodgers in the series with his tremendous all-round play.

Gregg took a deep breath after that close shave and went to work on Billy Johnson. The Yankee third baseman hit a ground ball into the hole between third and short—a tough "slot" chance. Reese scampered over, backhanded the ball, flipped to Stanky for one out. Stanky threw to Robinson to double up Johnson—and Gregg was out of it.

As Pee Wee trotted past Gregg on the way to the Dodger dugout, the pitcher gave his shortstop an affectionate smack on the shoulder.

"Thanks, Pee Wee," he grinned.

The Yankees picked up a second run in the fourth inning on a triple by Johnson and a double by Lindell. The Dodgers, meanwhile, were getting nowhere with Floyd Bevens. The Yankee pitcher was wild, but they couldn't get to him for a hit.

In the fifth Bevens walked Jorgensen and Gregg. Stanky sacrificed them over and Reese came up. Pee Wee, trying to hit to right field, bounced into the hole between first and second. Stirnweiss was able to get to the ball and throw him out, but Jorgensen came in to score.

It was still 2–1 going into the bottom of the ninth. And Bevens hadn't given up a hit to the Dodgers yet. The fans were sitting on the edge of their seats. No pitcher in World Series history had ever pitched a no-hitter.

Bruce Edwards flied to left. Furillo drew Bevens' ninth walk, but Spider Jorgensen fouled to McQuinn. The Yankee pitcher was one out away from immortality. Playing all the percentages, manager Shotton sent little Al Gionfriddo in to run for Furillo, and Pete Reiser went up to bat for the Dodgers' fourth pitcher of the game, Hugh Casey.

Berra had been having a tough series with the Dodger base runners, and Shotton sent Gionfriddo down on the first pitch. Little Al made it easily as Berra threw badly to second. Manager Bucky Harris then made a very unorthodox move. He ordered Bevens to walk Reiser intentionally, though this put the potentially winning run on base. Shotton countered by sending Cookie Lavagetto up to hit for Stanky. There didn't seem to be any reason for this strategy, but Shotton admitted later it was just "a hunch."

It was a hunch to end all hunches. Cookie punched a double off the right field wall. Gionfriddo scored the tying run, and as the hysterical crowd screamed "Run! Run!" Eddie Miksis, Reiser's pinch runner, hustled around third and slid across the plate with the winning tally.

The Yankees just stood around on the field for a minute, not believing the game was over. One second Bevens had a no-hitter. The next he had not only lost that, but the game as well! It was Lavagetto's only hit of the series, and it didn't make Bevens any happier when a writer told him that it was the only base hit Cookie got to right field all season.

Shea came back to pitch the Yankees to a 2–1 victory in the fifth game, giving up only four hits. But Pee Wee still seemed to be a one-man plague to Joe DiMaggio. In the third inning he took another hit away from DiMag and converted it into a double play. Then in the ninth he repeated the performance.

After the game, DiMaggio said to a reporter, "If the

Dodgers had eight more guys like that Reese, we wouldn't have a chance."

Paced by Pee Wee's double, two singles, two runs batted in and two runs scored, the Dodgers evened the series at three games apiece with an 8–6 win. In the first inning, Stanky singled and Pee Wee doubled him home. In the sixth, with the Yankees ahead, 5–4, Reese topped off a four-run rally with his third hit, a single that again scored Stanky.

That, however, was the Dodgers' last gasp. They just didn't have the pitching. With Joe Page mopping up again in the seventh game, the Yankees won it, 5–2, and their eleventh World Series.

In forcing the Yankees to seven games, at least the Dodgers did not go down without honor. And Reese . . . well, Pee Wee led all the other Dodger hitters with a .304 series average. He got seven hits, stole three bases, fielded five double plays. Of the Dodger total of twenty-nine runs for the seven games, Pee Wee accounted for nine of them himself, scoring five and batting in four.

CHAPTER 13

Back in 1940, when the Dodgers were still in the process of transformation from the laughingstock of the league to the powerful organization they are today, two promising youngsters showed up in their Florida camp. One was Harold "Pee Wee" Reese, marbles champion; the other was Harold "Pistol Pete" Reiser, lover of cowboy movies. Before the 1940 season was over these two youngsters were to be known as the "Gold Dust Twins."

Pee Wee, the shortstop from Louisville, and Pete, a shortstop and sometimes outfielder from the Elmira club, were introduced to each other in Florida by Ted Mc-Grew, the scout who brought them both to Brooklyn.

"Harold, meet Harold," the jocular scout said. "Now you two guys get to know each other, because you'll both be around here a long time, or I miss my guess."

McGrew came pretty close to missing, at that.

When the Dodgers broke their Clearwater camp and started heading north to play exhibition games, Larry MacPhail went over the club's player roster with Leo Durocher.

"We might as well start cutting out some of the dead wood now, Leo," MacPhail said. "The guys we don't intend keeping we can start assigning to the minor league clubs."

"Good idea, Larry," Durocher conceded. "There's two kids here we're definitely going to keep. The rest we can start trimming easily enough."

"Who's the two guys?" MacPhail asked.

"Reese and Reiser."

MacPhail raised his eyebrows. "What's the big deal with Reese and Reiser?"

"What do you mean, what's the big deal with Reese and Reiser?" Durocher shot back. "You've seen them play. They're the best couple of prospects we've seen in years. We're lucky to have them!"

"Well, I'm not so sure," MacPhail hesitated. "I'll go along on Reese. We can use him to fill in for you at short this year. But I feel Reiser will be improved by having another season of minor league experience under his belt. Anyway, he's supposed to be a shortstop. And you've got Reese."

"I'm converting Reiser to an outfielder, Larry," Durocher protested.

"You can use one, all right," MacPhail conceded. "But Reiser's no outfielder. Not yet, anyway."

"True," Durocher said. "But I figured that this year I'd use him to fill in both in the infield and the outfield, then by next year he'd be ready to take over the outfield alone."

"So you're only arguing my point," MacPhail persisted. "Let's send him down for another year and let him play the outfield down there. Why let him make his mistakes with us?"

"Because this guy can hit and run like Ty Cobb."

MacPhail snorted derisively. "Every year some kid

comes up and hits and runs like Ty Cobb. For two weeks. Then he's a bum."

Durocher shook his head. "Not this kid."

"You're darned right not this kid. Because we're sending him down for another year."

"I don't know, Larry, I'd just about decided to keep him up with us," Durocher said.

"*You've* decided!" MacPhail exploded. "What do you mean, *you've* decided? Who's running this ball club, you or me?"

"Well, I'm the manager, ain't I?"

"In about five minutes you won't be nothing, if you don't listen to my orders," MacPhail stormed.

"I'll listen as soon as you give me the okay to keep Reiser," Durocher raged right back.

"I'll give you no such thing! Reiser's going to Montreal. And that's final!"

Durocher pounded his fist on MacPhail's desk. "Reiser's going to play for the Dodgers this year!"

MacPhail leaped from his chair. "I warned you, Durocher! Now get out of here and tell Reiser to pack his bags. Then you can pack your own! You're through!"

"That's okay by me," Durocher snapped, and stormed from the room.

Well, just as it turned out a couple of dozen times during their stormy relationship, the firing of Durocher didn't stick. But it was different with Pete Reiser. He was sent to Montreal, then to Elmira after a few games.

But Durocher, at least, had the satisfaction of seeing Reiser called up midway through the 1940 season when the Dodgers were in trouble.

Pee Wee Reese was overjoyed when his friend reported

back to the club. "I told you they couldn't keep you down there," Pee Wee said to Reiser, punching him playfully on the shoulder. "We need you on this team, Pete. You'll murder this league."

"I sure hope I stick this time, Pee Wee," Reiser said. "I'd like to keep playing on the same team with you."

"Same here, Pete. You're an okay guy."

"Say listen, Pee Wee," Reiser said, "where do you stay when we're playing at home?"

"A hotel downtown where most of the single guys stay. Why, Pete, got an idea?"

"Yeah, Pee Wee, kind of. I was wondering, how about us finding some nice apartment in Brooklyn, not far from Ebbets Field? Wouldn't it be more comfortable than living in a hotel room?"

"Hey, that's not a bad idea, Pete," Reese said. "Tell you what, first rainout we get—or some morning, if we can get up early enough—let's take a look around. We can buy the Brooklyn *Eagle;* they've got lots of apartment ads."

"Great," the other agreed. "And listen, let's see if we can be roomies on the road, too, hey?"

Pee Wee stuck his hand out. "You got yourself a deal, partner."

So one morning the two youngsters—Reese, who was barely twenty-one, and Reiser, who was twenty, scurried about Brooklyn, apartment hunting like a couple of eager college freshmen their first time away from home. They found one soon enough, and became roommates on the road too, cementing a friendship that became unique in baseball. Most baseball players, understandably, consider themselves merely transients in their highly competitive game, and deep, personal relationships like Reese and Reiser's were naturally a rarity.

The "Gold Dust Twins" was an appropriate tag for the two friends. You never saw one of them without the other, and on the field they cheered each other on in a way that was contagious to the team as a whole. It gave the Dodgers a tremendous lift—the way Pee Wee and Pete stood together during the years Reiser played with Brooklyn.

In a way they were a strange combination. Pee Wee, the boyish, happy-go-lucky kid, and Reiser, kind of somber and moody. According to many ballplayers, Reiser was a hard man to get along with. But Pete and Pee Wee got along perfectly together.

During the spring training season of 1942, Dorothy Walton, Reese's girl and Ruth Hurst, Reiser's fiancée visited the Dodger's Daytona Beach camp. Immediately the couples started double dating.

"Dorothy," Pee Wee said, when he introduced her to Reiser for the first time, "I want you to meet the greatest guy I've ever known."

"You took the words right out of my mouth, Pee Wee," said Reiser, introducing his fiancée.

The romance of these youngsters was the topic of much good-natured kidding among the older players in the club. "Ah, flaming youth," was a typical comment by one of the players, as the two couples would drive off on a date. "Off they go to spend another exciting evening seeing a cowboy picture."

"Yeah," said another, "I'll bet they've seen every movie in town at least twice. I think they go just so's they can hold hands in the dark."

"Hey, Leo," said a third player to manager Durocher. "Don't you think you ought to go along as a chaperon? Those guys might eat too much popcorn or something."

"Wise guys," growled Durocher. "If you birds'd live more like those kids instead of running around all the time, you might last a little longer in this league."

"Hah! Look who's talkin'," laughed one of the Dodgers, but Durocher glared at him and he shut up suddenly.

The Florida moon must have had a little extra something that spring, for one evening while the four were having dinner, Pee Wee spoke up:

"Pete, Ruth," he said, "Dorothy and I want you two to be the first to know we're going to get married Sunday."

"No kidding!" Reiser exclaimed. "You lucky dog! Dotty's too good for you."

"I'm so happy for you, Dorothy," Ruth said.

"We're going over to City Hall to get a license tomorrow morning," Pee Wee said. "Want to drive over with us?"

"Sure, Pee Wee," Reiser said.

"And Harold and I would like you and Ruth to stand up for us on Sunday," Dorothy added. "Would you?"

"We'd never forgive you if you asked anybody else," said Reiser seriously.

The next morning, as the two couples were driving to the City Hall, Reiser said, with deliberate casualness, "You know, Pee Wee, Ruth and I were talking, and we figured as long as we're going down to the license bureau with you, we may as well take one out, too."

"Pete! Why, you son of a gun! That's terrific!" exclaimed Reese.

"We figured on having the ceremony on Monday, Pee Wee, so you and Dorothy can stand up for us."

"You bet, Pete," Pee Wee said. Then, he added, "Well, I guess you'd have to call today killing two ballplayers with one stone, eh, folks?"

And they all laughed.

Though the friendship of these two promising young ballplayers continued on its even way, their baseball careers began to take divergent paths in 1942. Reese, after his rocky 1941 season, was beginning to settle down and play the kind of ball that had always been expected of him. For Reiser, the batting champ and 1941 Rookie of the Year, 1942 was the beginning of a long, unlucky road downhill.

Reiser was hitting at a .380 clip until July 12th, when he ran full speed into the center field wall at Sportsman's Park chasing a fly ball hit by the Cardinal's Enos Slaughter. Pete bounded off the wall as if it were made of rubber, but some instinct enabled him to stagger after the ball and throw it into the infield before he collapsed. Reese took the throw-in and threw home, too late, however, to get Slaughter, then raced out to center field to his stricken friend.

Reiser was out of the line-up only a few days, but headaches, backaches and double vision haunted him, and he played mediocre ball the rest of the reason.

Reiser went into the Army and Reese into the Navy the following winter. And according to some misinformed sources, this started the breakup of their friendship. Reiser, the story went, was more morose than ever after his accident, and Pee Wee's long cheery letters to him while they were in service went unanswered.

When the story got back to Reese after both men had returned to the Dodgers in 1946, his usually cheerful face became cloudy. "I don't know who started that rumor," Pee Wee said angrily. "But it's a downright lie. If anything, I was the guy who didn't answer Pete's letters. My wife'll tell you I'm the world's worst letter writer. I was so slow in answering letters that when I was in the Pacific Pete used to call Dorothy and my mother whenever he'd get a letter from me, because he knew they might not have heard anything for a few days."

"That's true," Dorothy Reese said. "Pete stayed in the States, you know, because of that accident he had in St. Louis. He called us regularly in Louisville, and when he'd get a furlough he and Ruth would make a point of visiting us for a while. Why, both Pete's mother and Harold's have always treated them like they were brothers."

Nevertheless reports of a bust-up between the two friends drifted into print year after year, especially when Reiser began feuding with the Dodgers' front office.

That started in the spring of 1946, when the raids by the Mexican League had baseball owners worried. Reiser, one of the top players in the league before entering service, was one of those who received a fabulous offer from the Mexicans. When he learned about the offer, Branch Rickey pleaded with Reiser to stay with the Dodgers. And he promised him "substantial compensation."

According to Reiser, until Leo Durocher put the pressure on Rickey later that year, the Mahatma hadn't come through with a dime.

Reiser always had trouble with Rickey on the matter of compensation. "I don't know what it is with that guy,"

Reiser said to Reese one spring. "He always promises me bonuses and increases, but when it comes time to pay off he throws some fancy mathematics at me and I wind up with less than I'd figured on getting."

Reiser's troubles along those lines weren't helped any by his series of injuries, and in 1947, when he cracked into the wall at Ebbets Field chasing another fly ball, he was out for more than a month. He hit .309 that year, but actually, except for the 1941 season, Reiser never really had a great year.

The friction between Reiser and the Brooklyn front office reached its bitter climax in 1948, when he was used in only sixty-four games, and was constantly being shifted between the outfield and third base. This angered Reiser and he began popping off to the writers about the way the Dodgers were treating him. And the Reese–Reiser split-up rumors started again when one writer claimed that Pee Wee, always a great competitor, had accused Reiser of sulking on the field and playing indifferent ball.

The inevitable happened after the 1948 season: Pete Reiser was traded to the Boston Braves. That separated him from Reese but, despite all the stories, that did not end their friendship.

"Anybody that says Pete Reiser and I ever had an argument is a liar," Reese said, when he learned of the trade. "Pete's the best friend I've got in baseball. And he always will be. But Pete asked to be traded—in print. You can't do that and not expect to get action. I'll tell you guys something," Pee Wee said to his interviewers. "Two weeks before he was traded I told Pete that if the Dodgers traded him, I hoped they'd trade me with him. That's how I love that guy," he said fiercely.

"And I hope he hits .500 at Boston," Pee Wee added. "But not against the Dodgers, of course," he finished, smiling.

After the trade, the two men met again for the first time when the Dodgers played the Braves in an exhibition game the following spring. They had dinner together, talked over old times and wished each other the best of luck.

The next day, Reiser drew a walk on his first trip to the plate. The next batter grounded to Jackie Robinson, who flipped over to Pee Wee for the force-out on Reiser. But before Pee Wee could throw back to first for a double play, he was sent spinning into the dirt by Reiser's slide. Pete dusted himself off and trotted back to the bench without a word. Then he turned and he and Pee Wee just looked at each other. Finally Reiser grinned, stuck out his chest and pointed to the letters on his uniform. His meaning was clear: "I'm with the Braves now; you're with the Dodgers."

Later, in the Dodgers' clubhouse, Reese was going over the incident with the baseball writers. "I guess it's true," Pee Wee said sadly, as if up until that minute he hadn't really believed it.

CHAPTER **14**

On the morning of December 5, 1947, the following announcement was released by the Dodgers:

> The 1947 contract of Leo Durocher has been renewed for 1948 by the Brooklyn Baseball Club.
>
> BRANCH RICKEY

So Durocher, after his year in exile, was given the reins again at Ebbets Field. But only temporarily, as it turned out. The team Durocher took over was far from being the pennant-winning combination of the year before. Stanky was traded, Robinson was overweight and ineffective, the pitchers couldn't pitch and the hitters weren't hitting. As the Dodgers plummeted to the second division and stayed there into July, only Pee Wee Reese was playing his usual game.

When the season was just two weeks old, Pee Wee was signally honored. On April 28th, the Columbia Broadcasting System devoted an entire hour-long program to his life story. Prominent baseball men and Reese's early tutors in Louisville appeared on the program. Men like Ralph Kimmel, Pee Wee's high school coach; Keith Sparks, coach of the New Covenant Church team; and Ted McGrew, the scout who discovered him—all gave testimony to Reese's devotion to the game and to his qualities as a regular guy.

As one baseball writer put it the next day, "One thing about Pee Wee—though he's probably the most embarrassed guy on earth right now on account of last night's broadcast, he doesn't have to start setting out to justify all the nice things said about him. He's already done that in the years he's been a member of the Dodgers. And if we know Pee Wee, he'll go on being what he is, a great ballplayer and a great guy, without giving a thought to being either."

It was a shame, in a way, that this testimonial to Reese had to come when the Dodgers were having their worst season in years. Try as Durocher would, he couldn't get the Dodgers out of the second division. Coming off a pennant year, this put Durocher in an impossible position in Brooklyn. But he wouldn't resign. And Branch Rickey didn't want to fire him.

When the problem was finally resolved, the solution caused an uproar in New York City that was good enough for a week of sports page headlines.

Durocher was in Montreal checking on some Dodger farm talent, when he was ordered to report back to Brooklyn. When he arrived at the Dodgers' offices on Montague Street, he found Branch Rickey waiting for him.

After discussing in general the plight of the Dodgers, Rickey came to the point.

"Leo," Rickey said, puffing on a cigar, "I had a very enlightening chat with Horace Stoneham the other day."

Durocher waited for Rickey to go on.

"He'd like you to come over and manage the Giants."

"What did you tell him?" Durocher asked.

"I told him I'd speak to you about it."

"Does that mean I'm fired?"

Rickey shifted uncomfortably in his chair. "Not at all, Leo. I think you will agree however, that we are both in an unenviable position right now. You, in particular, might be considered to be on the spot. It may well be, Leo, that your future will be improved with the Giants. It will be a fresh start for you, a new challenge."

"That's all I wanted to know," Durocher said. "I'll phone you as soon as I arrange things with Stoneham."

The consternation among both Dodger and Giant fans when the news was announced may well be imagined. Followers of both teams are famous for being bitter antagonists against each other. Leo Durocher, manager of the New York Giants? For Dodger fans, it was pure treason. And Giant fans were being asked to accept a sworn enemy as a brother.

The players on both teams were also subject to a somewhat milder reaction. True, they were professional ballplayers. But Leo Durocher was never the kind of manager who left either his own men or the opposition in a state of neutrality.

When Rickey announced that Burt Shotton, who managed the Dodgers to their 1947 pennant, was being brought back to finish out the 1948 season, the Dodger players were asked for comment. Some, naturally, didn't care to be quoted in print. Jackie Robinson, for one, said he was glad to hear of Shotton's return. Robbie had come to the Dodgers when Shotton was in command, and the two had hit it off well.

Pee Wee Reese pulled no punches. "I'm a Durocher man," he stated.

This was not exactly a prudent remark, in view of Shotton's return. But nobody who knew Reese—and that included Shotton himself—expected Pee Wee's answer to be any different. After all, Reese had come to the Dodgers as a scared kid from Louisville. And Durocher could have made things tough for the youngster who was to take over his job as shortstop.

Instead, Durocher had been like a father to Reese, as Pee Wee himself often said. So it was only to be expected that Reese express himself as he had, and Shotton respected him for his loyalty.

Several weeks later, when the Dodgers had passed the Giants in the league standings, a sports writer well known for his anti-Durocher sentiments approached Pee Wee. "How do you think the Giants are going to make out under Durocher?" the writer asked.

"Well, you can throw out this year," Reese replied. "But next year, and from then on, they're going to be tough. They've got to get better. Leo's a great manager."

When the sports writer sniffed derisively, Pee Wee said, "You don't like Durocher, do you? As a person, I mean? Well, you know, Billy Herman hated him, too, and with better reason than you have. But I've spoken to Billy about Leo several times, and he told me he thought Durocher was one of the best managers baseball ever had. He ranked Leo right behind Joe McCarthy. Coming from Billy, I always thought that was the highest compliment Durocher could be paid. And that's the way I think, too," Reese added. "Durocher's a wonderful manager."

"Then how do you account for the fact that while the Dodgers were floundering around the second division for the first half of the season, you started playing winning ball when Shotton took over?" the writer asked.

"One of the big factors was that we didn't have Stanky at second base to start the season. So we had to experiment with the infield, playing the guys in unfamiliar positions. Then, too, Robinson wasn't in good shape physically. We needed a catcher. Some of the pitchers weren't going right. Those things weren't Leo's fault. When we got Roy Campanella up from St. Paul, moved Hodges to first and Robinson to second, we began to come around. Without meaning to take anything away from Shotton," Reese finished, "you've got to remember this—that we were on a five-game winning streak when Durocher left."

As Shotton took over the club, the Dodgers began moving slowly up the ladder. For a brief while in August they even held the league lead. But they dropped downward again, and stayed down, winding up third, behind Boston and St. Louis.

Pee Wee hit .274 that year and batted in seventy-five runs. He led National League shortstops in put-outs and double plays, and once again was named to the All-Star team. This time, however, he was not, as previously, rated second-string behind Eddie Miller of Boston or Marty Marion of St. Louis. This time he was the National League's starting shortstop for the annual classic. There was no doubt now about who was Mr. Shortstop.

In January of 1949, Branch Rickey paid an unexpected call on Pee Wee Reese at the latter's home in Louisville. "I'm out in this part of the country on a business trip, Pee Wee," Rickey said to his surprised shortstop, "so I thought I'd drop by for a little chat."

Wise in the ways of the Dodgers' boss, Reese knew Rickey wasn't the man to stop by "for a chat." Not with the relentless pace of work Rickey set for himself. No, if he had gone to the trouble of stopping off in Louisville, it was to discuss some serious business.

After some moments of the usual Rickey oratory, the Mahatma came to the real reason for his visit. "Pee Wee," he said, "sometime during the next baseball season you will be thirty years old. Not a young man by baseball standards. Already you are being talked of as 'the last of the old Dodgers.' "

Reese smiled. "I didn't think it showed yet."

Rickey took out a fresh cigar, bit off the tip, lit it and sent a cloud of blue smoke spiraling to the ceiling of Pee Wee and Dorothy's comfortable living room. "I'm glad it does show," he said. "And that's what brings me here today. Because I'd like to think of you as the first of the new Dodgers."

"How do you mean, B. R.?" Reese asked.

"Well, as you probably know, since Dolph Camilli left the Dodgers in 1943, the team has been without a captain. I'd like you to be the team captain for 1949."

Reese thought a long time before answering. "I'm flattered, of course, Branch," he said. "But I don't think I'm the man for the job. In fact, I don't even think I want it."

Rickey looked startled. "Why not?"

"Well, my reasons are kind of mixed up, I guess. For one thing, I remember the way it was with Stanky. He sort of took over the infield unofficially, you know. He was just that kind of player. A real spark plug. A holler guy. But some of the players resented his attempt at authority. I wouldn't want any of the guys to feel that way about me, or feel that I was showboating or anything like that."

Rickey was chewing his cigar energetically now. There was nothing he liked better than the challenge of converting a mind with an opinion different from his own. "But you wouldn't be in that position, Pee Wee. You'd be acting with my expressed authority on the field. An official captain."

"Even then I'm not sure I'd like the idea," Reese persisted. "I don't know that I want to order the other fellows around. You know, the year I first broke in with the Dodgers, Durocher wanted me to do that. But I looked around at men like Camilli and Lavagetto, and I told Durocher, 'How do you expect me to order around men like that?' "

Rickey leaned back in his chair and smiled—like a chess player who had just seen his opponent fall into the trap that was laid by his opening gambit. "Ah, that is precisely my point," he said. "The Camillis and the Lavagettoes, and yes, the Stankys, too, are no longer here. You are not only the oldest player on the Dodgers in point of service, but you are also the most mature. It is not only I who respect you, your ability and your judgment. It is the players as well. That's why, Pee Wee, you are the logical one to hold this team together."

Since it was difficult for Reese to refute the logic of Rickey's arguments, with some misgivings he accepted the appointment. He also accepted a new 1949 contract that Rickey had brought along, which called for twenty-four thousand dollars, including the extra five hundred dollars a player gets for serving as team captain. The contract not only made Reese the highest paid of the National

League shortstops at that time, it made him one of the highest paid Dodgers of all time.

Pee Wee would have stepped into his new role as captain much less gingerly had he known of the players' reaction to his appointment. "Don't print this," one Dodger veteran told a sports writer, "because it would only embarrass Pee Wee. But there's not one of us who has any gripe about his being captain. Everybody on this club knows Pee Wee's a real team man. Nobody puts more heart into the game than he does. And we know he's not going to be any front office stooge, either."

Reese had his chance to prove that point quickly enough. When the players felt that two workouts a day in spring training were too much, they went to Pee Wee with their complaint. Reese agreed and promptly straightened the matter out with manager Shotton.

The choice of Pee Wee for team captain promptly led to the speculation that he was being groomed to succeed Shotton as the Dodgers' pilot. For it was no secret that the sixty-three-year-old manager had returned to Brooklyn only as a special favor to Rickey. As soon as the Dodgers could find a good manager to replace him, Shotton was ready to go back to his semiretirement in Florida.

"How about it, Pee Wee?" the sports writers began asking Reese at the Dodgers' camp in Vero Beach, Florida. "You given much thought to being a manager?"

"Not a bit," Reese answered seriously. "I'm too young yet. Heck, I've got a good six or seven years of playing shortstop ahead of me. Maybe then I'll start thinking about it. But not now."

Pee Wee shortly had other problems to think about. In

an exhibition game against the Athletics at West Palm Beach, Pee Wee suddenly pulled up lame as he rounded second base. Reese limped off the field complaining of a severe pain in his groin. When the soreness persisted, Reese decided to remain on the bench for a few days, figuring on a pulled muscle.

When the Dodgers began a series of exhibition games in Texas, Pee Wee put himself back in the line-up. He played nine innings, but complained of the soreness again. "It doesn't hurt when I swing a bat," he told Shotton. "But I can't make quick starts or run bases properly without feeling pain."

An examination revealed an enlarged gland in the groin, and a possible hernia. The following day, however, another examination by a different doctor brought a diagnosis of just a pulled muscle. Which proved, as one sports writer later said, that "doctors are, after all, just about as infallible as umpires."

The year 1949 turned out to be one of those "next years" Brooklyn fans always seem to be waiting for. But the pennant didn't come to Ebbets Field until the very last day of the season, and not without its frights—especially for Pee Wee Reese.

Despite the constant pain in his groin and right leg, Pee Wee stayed in the line-up without a break. As the season wore on, he came to accept his being captain as a matter of fact, finding that his fears of friction with his teammates were unfounded. They accepted him without question as their liaison man between the team and the front office and their leader on the field.

And in his own quiet way, Pee Wee made the team run smoothly. Because the men were certain of his fairness, he was able to smooth over the petty irritations and squabbles that are bound to come about during the heat of a pennant fight.

During the dog days of August, one of the players came to Reese before the start of the afternoon's game. "Pee Wee," he said, "I just don't feel right. I haven't been hitting and my fielding's getting sloppy and I can't seem to work my way out of it."

"You think a couple of days on the bench'll give you your wind back?" Pee Wee asked.

"Just one day," the player pleaded. "One day off and I know I'll be able to pull myself together."

Reese nodded. "I'll speak to Shotton."

Later, when the Dodger manager showed Pee Wee the day's starting line-up, the captain pointed to one name on the list. "Not him today, Burt. He needs a day off, but he won't ask you for it."

Shotton looked at Pee Wee evenly. "He isn't the only one who needs a day off and won't ask for it. I know how it hurts you to play, Pee Wee. You can't hide that wince of pain when you start running for a ball."

Reese shrugged. "Not everybody's the same, Burt. It's no rap at the guy that he needs a day off."

"You really think it'll do him any good?"

"It'll make his mind easier," Reese said. "That's all he needs to straighten himself out."

Shotton agreed. If Reese thought the man needed a day off, then he really did need it, the manager knew.

On Sunday, September 11th, with the Dodgers a game and a half behind the Cardinals, they came near being knocked out of the pennant race with one pitch. Locked in a close game with the Giants, they suddenly erupted against pitcher Larry Jansen in the seventh inning to break the game wide open.

Three straight hits and a walk brought in one run and loaded the bases. Up stepped Carl Furillo, and out of the ball park went Jansen's first pitch for a grand slam home run.

The Giant hurler stomped around the mound in disgust. Then the Dodgers' pitcher Carl Erskine rubbed salt in Jansen's wound by clouting a single to left. He came down with his pitch to Pee Wee. As the ball neared the plate, Pee Wee suddenly threw his arms over his head and fell away. But the inside pitch hit him. From the stands it looked as if the ball had crashed into his head, but as he ducked away he had been fortunate enough to stick his left arm in front of his face. The ball bounced off his elbow.

It was a lucky break, the arm getting hit instead of his face, but the damage seemed serious enough. There was no fracture, but the elbow was severely bruised, and the doctors figured it would be a week before Reese could play again. They hadn't figured on Pee Wee's courage, however.

Two days later, when the Dodgers opened a crucial western swing at Cincinnati, Pee Wee put himself back into the line-up. When he came up for his first time at bat against pitcher Howie Fox, Pee Wee struck out. As he swung futilely at the third strike he winced with pain and grabbed instinctively at his injured elbow. His next time up Pee Wee hit a two-and-two pitch against the fence for a double.

That evening, Pee Wee had dinner with his widowed mother, who had come up from Louisville to see her son play. "Harold," she said to Pee Wee, "it seemed to me you hurt yourself every time you swung today."

"I did, Mom," Pee Wee admitted. "I got a sharp pain in that elbow I hurt."

"Well, then, you shouldn't have played today, you know," his mother said.

"Mom," Pee Wee explained, "I'm the captain of the team. I've got to play."

But at that time not even Pee Wee's mother was aware that he had a far more serious concern on his mind than his injured elbow. When Pee Wee left his home in Brooklyn the day before, his daughter Barbara had taken ill. It was during a serious polio scare in New York, and naturally Pee Wee and his wife were apprehensive.

Without telling anyone on the team about the danger, Pee Wee continued on the road trip, phoning New York continually for reports on his daughter's illness. She did contract polio, but fortunately it was diagnosed quickly, and under the expert care of pediatrician Dr. Morris Steiner, who had cared for her since birth, the disease was carefully controlled. Today Barbara is a perfectly normal young girl of twelve.

Two weeks later, the Dodgers returned from a triumphal western tour with a one-game lead. Only two games against the Phillies remained before sewing up the pennant. They won the first game, but the Cardinals won their game, too. The Cardinals also won their last game of the season, and Brooklyn had to win its final game or wind up in a tie.

While the final score of the Cardinals' game loomed on the scoreboard, the Dodgers were up to their ears in a battle with the Phillies. Pitchers on both sides were shelled from the mound as fast as they came in, and at the end of the regulation nine innings the score was tied, 7–7.

Dodger players and Dodger fans alike remembered 1946, when the Dodgers and Cardinals tied for the pennant, and the Red Birds beat Brooklyn two straight to win the play-off. They were in no mood for a repeat performance of that kind. So the Dodgers went out and beat the Phillies in the tenth inning, 9–7, and the pennant had come again to Ebbets Field.

For the third straight time, the Dodgers' opponents in the World Series were the New York Yankees. And since 1955 was still six years away, the Yankees beat the Dodgers with their usual aplomb. It took them only five games this time.

It was not a hitter's series, the Yankees winding up as a team with a .226 average, the Dodgers with a .210. But Reese led both teams in hitting with a .316 average, and he also hit his first World Series home run.

Two months after the series furor had died down, Jackie Robinson became the first Negro to receive the highest honor baseball can bestow. He was voted the Most Valuable Player in the National League in the annual poll conducted by the Baseball Writers Association of America.

Robinson's acceptance speech was very simple. He was honored—and proud. But if the selection had been up to him, well, "I'd have picked Pee Wee as the most valuable player on our club," Robinson said.

Reese had placed fifth in the balloting. Despite his continuous abdominal pains, his arm injury and the illness of his daughter, Pee Wee managed to bat .279, hit sixteen home runs—more than he had ever hit before—and twenty-seven doubles. He also wound up leading the league in runs scored, put-outs and fielding average. Not a bad year for the "last of the old Dodgers."

CHAPTER 15

There has always been considerable speculation among baseball men about when Pee Wee Reese stopped being the kid from Louisville and started being Pee Wee Reese the man. According to Leo Durocher, this event came about in 1946, when Pee Wee had returned from his Navy service. It was during a spring exhibition game in Daytona Beach.

There was a ground ball hit to Reese's right, into the hole between third and short. Pee Wee raced over, picked it up and with one smooth motion that made Durocher's eyes glow, threw the runner out at first.

When the inning was over, Reese trotted back to the dugout. He looked at Durocher and winked and his mouth parted in that little kid's grin of his. But Durocher knew, as he returned the wink and the grin, that despite that familiar boyish face, this wasn't the same kid that went away in 1942 to join the Navy.

As Pee Wee took his seat on the bench next to Durocher, the Dodger manager draped an arm around his shoulder. "Pee Wee," he said to Reese, "you went away to war a boy, you came back a man."

Maybe that really was the day Pee Wee Reese officially became a man in baseball. But Branch Rickey, who made Pee Wee field captain of the Dodgers in 1949, has a different idea.

According to Rickey, Pee Wee reached the full development of his baseball maturity with the coming of Jackie Robinson to Brooklyn. "What Reese did for Robinson," Rickey said, "what he did for himself, the Dodgers, for baseball generally and for the entire problem of human relations can never be overestimated. And the day finally came, in 1949, when I knew that Reese was ready to be the field leader of the Dodgers and the players' liaison with the front office."

Or perhaps it was during the 1949 World Series, the second game, to pin it down, that Reese showed he'd become a man. At least, that's the way it seems to Burt Shotton, who was managing the Dodgers then.

"Preacher Roe told me about it when the game was over," Shotton said. "Old Preach was pitching a whale of a game against the Yankees that day, leading them 1–0, and making them look silly swatting at the junk stuff he was feeding them. But in the eighth inning the Yanks get two men on, and there comes Henrich stepping up to the plate.

"Well, Preach remembers well enough that all Henrich did the day before was hit a home run in the ninth inning that beat us, 1–0. And though Preach was about the coldest fish ever when it came to pitching out of trouble, he had to admit he was a little edgy when Henrich dug himself in at the plate.

"All of a sudden Pee Wee calls time," Shotton went on. "And he walks slowly over to the mound. 'Preach,' he says, 'Let's you and me have a little talk.'

"'Sure thing, Pee Wee.' Roe answers him. 'What about?'

"'Heck, Preach. Anything at all. Hunting, fishing,

how's the weather in Arkansas. Just let's keep Henrich waiting up there and wondering how you're going to pitch to him,' Pee Wee says.

"Well," said Shotton, "I'm standing there on the steps of the dugout, watching them, and then I notice Pee Wee kind of turns to me and nods his head, ever so little. And I knew he was just letting me know that Roe was okay, that he hadn't lost his stuff or his confidence. Roe beat the Yankees, 1–0, of course.

"Yes, somehow I got the feeling then that Pee Wee was the kind of baseball man Mr. Rickey always said he would be."

As important as all these milestones in Pee Wee's career may be, however, it is on no less an authority than Pee Wee himself that the date for his emergence as a full-fledged ballplayer was probably May 4, 1950.

It happened in the fifth inning of a game in Chicago, Pee Wee's one thousandth game with the Dodgers, appropriately enough. The Dodgers were leading the Cubs, 9–0, and Reese had already collected two hits. On this trip to the plate, however, Pee Wee took a three-and-two pitch that umpire Babe Pinelli called strike three.

Reese whirled angrily on Pinelli. He said nothing, but glared at the umpire, and as he walked away he threw his bat high in the air. Pinelli's thumb went up right after the bat did, and Pee Wee Reese had been thrown out of the first ball game of his career. He walked back to the dugout and stood on the steps, his arms folded, still glaring at Pinelli. As coach Clyde Sukeforth started past Reese to argue his ejection with the umpire, Pee Wee put his arm out and stopped him.

"Let it be, Sukey," he said. "It's the first time. Maybe it makes me a man," he laughed.

The season wasn't a particularly successful one for the Dodgers—or for Pee Wee. It was the year of the Philadelphia "Whiz Kids," and Brooklyn finished second, beat out on the last day of the season. As for Pee Wee, he suffered a general letdown, batting only .260, his poorest year since returning from the Navy. It was peculiar, in a way, for he had expected a good season. In 1949, he had played through with a hernia and played well. Before the start of the 1950 season he had been operated on in Louisville for the injury, but he recovered in time to make the Dodgers' Florida training camp. Yet 1950 was one of Pee Wee's poorer years.

Meanwhile, there seemed to be little doubt in anyone's mind that Branch Rickey and Burt Shotton were figuring on Reese's taking over Shotton's manager's job in the near future. Reese seemed to be the natural choice. And, judging from one little conversation, there was probably some discussion of the matter between Shotton and Rickey.

It was a rainy night at Ebbets Field in July of 1950. The game had just been postponed and Shotton was sitting in his office under the stands, talking to a couple of the baseball writers.

Just then Reese stuck his head into the room, "Say, Burt, what do you tell these guys on a rainy night so they can earn their day's pay?"

"Come in and learn," Shotton replied. "So when I retire you'll know what to say."

The plans of all three men, however—if there were any such plans at all—became just wishful thinking shortly after the 1950 season came to a close. Branch Rickey bowed out of the Brooklyn organization and was replaced by Walter O'Malley, as president of the Dodgers. O'Malley immediately appointed Fresco Thompson and E. J. (Buzzy) Bavasi as his vice presidents.

There was no doubt from the first about where Burt Shotton stood in the new scheme of things. During the first week of reorganization, he wasn't even invited to the staff meetings. How this change of stewardship would affect Reese was still open to speculation.

Thompson and Bavasi were known to be enthusiastic supporters of Pee Wee. As far back as 1949, Bavasi had declared, "If they don't make that kid the manager they've sure been stringing him along for a long time."

President O'Malley, however, had other points to consider. "Frankly," he confided to a sports writer, "and strictly off the record for now, I can't take a chance on a new manager in my first year as president. I'll have to hire a manager with experience."

"That lets Pee Wee out, then," said the other.

"Yes," agreed O'Malley, "I'm afraid for the present that leaves Pee Wee out."

There was more than a little criticism leveled at the Dodgers' president when he announced that Charlie Dressen would manage the Dodgers in 1951. Many of the fans and writers wanted to know why the popular Reese had been by-passed for the job.

Typically, it was Pee Wee himself who got O'Malley neatly off the hook. "I think the burden of being a manager, especially a playing manager, would be too much for me now," he said. "I sincerely believe I have three years or more of playing ahead of me. I wouldn't want to jeopardize that."

As for Charlie Dressen, he couldn't have picked a worse year to start managing the Dodgers. They really blew the pennant in 1951, and in much more spectacular fashion than they did in 1942.

The Dodgers' line-up looked like a pennant-winning one when the season opened. There were Hodges at first, Robinson at second, Reese at short and Cox on third. The outfield had Furillo, Snider and Pafko. Roy Campanella was behind the plate and among the pitchers were Newcombe, Erskine, Labine, Branca and Roe.

By midsummer the pennant race seemed to be all over but the shouting. On August 11th the Dodgers had a lead of thirteen and a half games over the second-place Giants. What happened after that point no one seems to be able to explain, but the Giants put on a miraculous stretch drive that wound up in one of the most exciting climaxes in the history of baseball.

It took a little while for the fans to realize what was in the making, for while the Giants whittled away steadily at the Dodgers' lead, the gap appeared too wide ever to overcome. But on September 2nd, when they took on the Giants at the Polo Grounds, the Dodgers must have gotten their first uneasy feeling.

It wasn't just that they were soundly trounced by the Giants, 8–1, but there were a couple of oddities in the game that seemed to indicate which way the wind was blowing in the pennant race.

The first item was Don Mueller. The year before the Giants' outfielder had hit a total of seven home runs. All of a sudden in this one game he went wild and hit three of them.

Then there was what happened to Reese. Pee Wee was the only Dodger that day who was able to get to Sal Maglie, the Giant hurler. Of the Dodgers' eight hits, Pee Wee got three of them. But then Maglie put the jinx on Pee Wee.

Cal Abrams was on second and Carl Furillo on first, late in the game, when Pee Wee came up to the plate. He took aim at Maglie's first pitch and smashed a wicked line drive—right into Al Dark's glove. Dark whirled, flipped to second to double up Abrams. Then Stanky tagged out Furillo coming down from first. A neat triple play—and the last rally the Dodgers mustered that day.

That's the way it went the rest of the season. The Dodgers couldn't seem to do anything right; the Giants could do no wrong. On the last day of the season the Giants pulled a victory out of the fire at the last minute and the race ended in a tie.

So again the Dodgers were involved in a play-off for the pennant. The first game was played at Ebbets Field, and Maglie, the Dodgers' nemesis, beat them, 3–1. But the next day Clem Labine shut out the Polo Grounders to even up matters.

The final game of the play-off series was a perfect finish to an exciting pennant race. It had a storybook ending that would have been unbelievable in a work of fiction.

In that final game, Big Don Newcombe had outpitched Maglie all the way, and the Dodgers were leading, 4–1, going into the bottom half of the ninth inning. The pennant was only three outs away.

Al Dark led off for the Giants by singling into right

field. Mueller also singled to right, sending Dark to third. But Newcombe bore down and got Monte Irvin to foul to Hodges. Lockman doubled to left, scoring Dark and sending Mueller to third. Hartung came in to run for Mueller, who had twisted his leg sliding into the bag.

Now the score was 4–2, and the tying runs were on base. Charlie Dressen went out to the mound, spoke to Newcombe briefly, then waved Branca in from the bull pen. With that same motion, Dressen had also waved good-by to the pennant.

Branca shot a fast ball past Bobby Thomson for a strike. Branca threw another fast ball and Thomson sent it on a high arc into the left field stands for a home run, Hartung trotted across the plate, Lockman trotted across with a tying run and then came Thomson with the run that won the pennant for the Giants.

It was quite a blow for the Dodgers. The coveted pennant, securely in their grasp, had been snatched away with one swipe of Thomson's bat. "That was the only game of my career," Pee Wee Reese remarked a couple of years later, "that I refused to discuss in the clubhouse afterward. It was like a nightmare and I wanted to forget it as soon as possible."

About the only thing Pee Wee would want to remember about the entire year of 1951 was that he had his best season at the plate to date. He hit .286, batted in eighty-four runs, hit ten home runs and led the Dodgers in triples with eight.

CHAPTER 16

Bad news, the saying goes, comes in a cluster of three, and since baseball players are notoriously superstitious, the Dodgers were inclined to be apprehensive about their fortunes in 1952.

Two years running the Dodgers had had the pennant snatched from them by a last ditch home run. In 1950 it was Dick Sisler's blast in the tenth inning of the final game of the season that saved the Phillies' one-run margin over the Dodgers. The next year it was Bobby Thomson's homer in the third game of the play-offs that put the Giants in the World Series and the Dodgers in the dumps. With a history of that kind of luck, who could blame the Dodgers for wondering and worrying?

They were sitting around in the locker room at Ebbets Field discussing it before their exhibition game with the Yankees prior to opening day. The scene was getting to be a familiar one by now. There was Pee Wee Reese, in his baseball pants and sweat shirt, puffing away placidly on an old briar pipe. Around "the little Colonel," as Kentucky-born Pee Wee had begun to be called, were clustered a number of the other players, gathered to talk things over with their captain.

"I guess we're just the unluckiest team in baseball," sighed one of the players.

"I know what you mean," said Reese. "But there's more to it than just saying you're unlucky."

"But look," said the other. "In '50 and '51 we got squeezed out by one game—and at the last minute, too. I'll bet if you go over some of the games those years you'll find that just one break the other way, somewhere along the line, and we'd have won the pennant."

"If you want to figure that way," Reese said, "then you've got to take the games we won by breaks. Maybe by the time you get through adding and subtracting, we wouldn't even have come close."

"Well, look at this year," persisted the player. "Before we even get started we lose Newcombe. He's maybe our best pitcher—and the Army takes him."

Pee Wee nodded. "That's tough on us, all right. But the Army also took Willie Mays from the Giants and Chet Nichols from the Braves. Maybe that kind of evens the score."

The exasperated player threw up his hands. "Whose side are you on, anyway?" he asked Reese.

Reese laughed. "I know what you're trying to get at, and maybe you're even right. But you've got to figure baseball is made up of breaks, good and bad, and that you're going to get your share of both. The only thing you can do then is forget about them and try to win the game you're playing that day. And what we've got to remember is this: The game you lose the first week of the season hurts just as much as losing the last game of the season when you blow the pennant by one game."

On the Dodger bench, meanwhile, as Reese was haranguing the Brooklyn players, voluble manager Charlie Dressen was sizing up the team for the writers.

"We won't blow this pennant," confided Dressen, who seemed to live most of his baseball life at the end of a limb. "We're set at every position. Losing Newcombe's going to hurt, but we've got a couple of youngsters up who may be able to make up for him, Joe Black and Johnny Podres."

"How about the infield, Charlie?" inquired a writer.

"What about it?" responded Dressen. "It's the best in baseball."

"Well, Reese'll be thirty-three in a couple of months. That's a tough age to be hopping around at shortstop. Maybe he's not the player he used to be."

"No, he's not," said Dressen. "He's better. Oh, he's lost a little of his speed, I guess. And he don't throw as hard as he used to. But he's more than made up for that by his smartness. In the field and at bat, he's much more an artist now than he ever was.

"In one way he's still the same Reese, though," added Dressen with a grin. "He still can't make the sacrifice bunt. I mean when you've got to stand there and give yourself up. When Pee Wee does it he pops up. He always has. The funny thing is, though, when he bunts for a hit he's one of the greatest."

"We can assume then," said one of the sports writers, "that you plan no changes with Pee Wee this year?"

Dressen nodded. "All I've done with Pee Wee is encourage him to swing. In the past he's had the habit of taking too many third strikes."

"It's true," Pee Wee admitted ruefully when he heard of Dressen's comment. "Taking that third strike's my worst habit."

"Dixie Walker used to say you were the greatest hitter

in baseball," said a sports writer. "Because you only got one swing. You always seemed to wait till they called two strikes on you before you took your cut."

Reese grinned. "I never heard that one before. But one of the umpires—I forget who it was, Goetz or somebody—once said to me, 'Pee Wee, why don't we speed things up by automatically giving you two strikes when you come up?'

"There's a good reason why I got into the habit, though," said Pee Wee. "It started when I became a lead-off man in the line-up. When you lead off, you know, the idea is to get on base, so sometimes you let a good pitch go because you're trying to work the pitcher for a walk. Then again, during the game you come up to bat right after the pitcher, unless he made the last out the inning before. So you wait again, because if you hit the first pitch, say, and are out, your pitcher won't have any time to rest after batting before he has to go to the mound again.

"This year, with Dressen figuring on me hitting second most of the time, maybe I'll be able to cut out taking those third strikes."

But the way Pee Wee started the 1952 season, it seemed that Dressen would have been wiser to let well enough alone with Reese's hitting. Maybe he wasn't taking third strikes so much, but at the same time, he wasn't hitting anything but pop flies for the first couple of months.

Pee Wee's slump was climaxed on April 22nd, in the first game of a double header against the Braves at Ebbets Field. The Dodgers were leading in the eighth inning, 1–0. The bases were loaded and Pee Wee, who was on deck, stood up, a couple of bats in his hand. Suddenly

Dressen called him back to the bench and sent George Shuba up to pinch-hit for him.

The twenty-five thousand fans at Ebbets Field, together with countless thousands more watching their television screens at home, witnessed a memorable event. The usually mild-mannered, loyal Reese lost his temper and slammed the bats against the dugout as he took his seat on the bench.

The Dodger fans on hand didn't like the idea of seeing their popular shortstop taken out of the game, and several loud boos came down from the stands. And when Shuba struck out, the hoots and catcalls from the crowd stung Dressen's ears for the rest of the game.

But Pee Wee was quick to apologize for his action between games of the double-header. "Of course I was mad," he told the sports writers. "Every ballplayer likes to get up there and hit in the clutch. But I was wrong. I haven't been hitting a lick—and after all, the manager is the boss.

"I apologized to Charlie and really felt sorry for him when the fans started booing him. He didn't deserve it. He was making a move he thought best destined to win."

Dressen, who rightly felt no need to defend his action, nevertheless explained the move. "Naturally," he said, "I wouldn't have lifted Reese if he were hitting right. He's one of the best clutch hitters in baseball. But he just hasn't been hitting. He's got one hit in his last seventeen times up. Of course, the fans got on me. They like Pee Wee. But you can't let the fans run your ball game."

Pee Wee's slump continued into the middle of May, and he was down to .216 before he began showing signs of awakening. He moved his average up to the more respectable area of .270 by June, then got hot in July. On the Dodgers' western swing that month they couldn't get Pee Wee out. And in Chicago one day, that figure of speech was translated literally by Pee Wee.

His first time up Pee Wee doubled, but his mates left him stranded. In the third inning he singled, scoring on Robinson's double. In the fifth Reese doubled and Robinson singled him home. In the sixth inning Pee Wee made it four-for-four, singling with the bases loaded to drive in two runs. He still wasn't through. He got up in the eighth and singled again, making it a five-for-five day as the Dodgers won, 12–2.

The Dodgers were riding smoothly along at the top of the league now, but remembering the previous two years, they still had their fingers crossed; everybody but manager Charlie Dressen, that is. Toward the end of the season a story appeared in the national magazines under Charlie's by-line, entitled "Why the Dodgers Won't Blow It Again."

The Brooklyn players howled. They would rather Dressen had let a black cat cross his path or had walked under a ladder than this defiance of superstition. Happily, the Dodgers didn't blow this pennant, but until that last game had gone into the record books nobody in the Brooklyn Dodger baseball organization could draw a deep breath.

Pee Wee closed out the season with a .272 batting average, leading the Dodgers again in triples with eight. More important, he led the league in stolen bases with thirty.

"For a thirty-three-year-old veteran," commented one baseball man, "those are significant statistics. When a player gets to be that age, the first sign that he's fading shows in his legs. Well, you don't hit eight triples and steal thirty bases without darn good legs.

"It looks like Pee Wee's going to be the Dodgers' perennial boy wonder," he added.

But they hadn't seen nothing yet, to paraphrase the old vaudeville line. Pee Wee really put on an exhibition in the World Series against the Yankees. It was in a losing cause, as the Yanks won the championship again. But the Dodgers drove them to seven games, with a healthy assist from their captain.

Dressen pulled a mild surprise for the first game of the fall classic. He started Joe Black on the mound. Joe, the Rookie of the Year, broke a record by appearing in fifty-six games for the Dodgers, winning fifteen and losing four. But except for the final week of the season he had only appeared in relief, and as such, had saved the Dodgers' lives.

Jackie Robinson started things against Yankee ace Allie Reynolds by homering into the left field stands in the second inning. But Gil McDougald got it back the same way in the third for the Yankees.

It was 1–1 until the last of the sixth. With one out, Reese singled, and Snider promptly hit one over the right field wall to make the score 3–1 Brooklyn. In the Yankees' eighth Woodling hit a pinch-hit triple and scored on Bauer's fly ball to make the score 3–2.

But Reese put the icing on for the Dodgers in their half of the eighth with a home run that made it 4–2 and the ball game.

Vic Raschi got the Yankees even in the second game,

beating the Dodgers and Carl Erskine, 7–1. Reese got one of the Dodgers three hits and scored their only run.

It was the Dodgers' turn again in the third game, with Roe beating Eddie Lopat, 5–3. The Yanks drew first blood in the second inning, but Reese tied matters in the third with a single after Furillo's double. In the fifth, the Dodgers made it 2–1. With two out, Reese singled, stole second and scored on Robinson's single. Then, with the Dodgers ahead, 3–2, in the ninth, Pee Wee started a two-run rally with his third single. That made it 5–2, nullifying a pinch-hit home run by Johnny Mize in the bottom of the ninth for the Yankees.

The seesaw went the other way again in the fourth game, Reynolds gaining revenge on Black with a 2–0 shutout of the Dodgers. Brooklyn got only four singles off Reynolds. Reese accounted for two of them.

In the fifth game the Yankees rocked Erskine for five runs in their half of the fifth, but Carl settled down after that and retired the last nineteen Yankees in a row. Meanwhile, the Dodgers tied the score in the seventh and won it in the eleventh inning on a double by Snider.

Vic Raschi finally silenced Pee Wee in the sixth game, for the first time in the series. And the Yankees tied things for the third time, making it three games apiece.

Joe Black and Eddie Lopat went at each other for the final game. The Yankees picked up a run in the fourth, but the Dodgers got it back in their half. In the fifth the Yankees made the score 2–1, but again the Dodgers evened things up as Billy Cox doubled and Reese, that man again, singled Billy home.

That, however, was all the scoring for the Dodgers, while the Yankees added single runs in the sixth and seventh to take the series, their fourth straight from Brooklyn.

Brooklyn's last gasp came in the seventh inning of that seventh game. Raschi, who had replaced the arm-weary Reynolds, walked Furillo to start the inning. Rocky Nelson popped up, but Billy Cox singled, with Reese walking, to load the bases.

With the left-hand-hitting Snider up, Casey Stengel called in his southpaw reliever Bob Kuzava to replace Raschi. Kuzava went to three-and-two on Snider, then got Duke on a pop-up.

Up came Jackie Robinson, and again Kuzava went three balls and two strikes. And again Kuzava got the hitter to pop up. Jackie lifted the ball high into the air to the left of the mound. It was clearly first baseman Joe Collins' ball, but he seemed to be losing it. While Kuzava stood on the mound as if hypnotized, second baseman Billy Martin made a mad dash in from second and grabbed the ball knee high on the dead run.

Furillo and Cox had already crossed the plate and Pee Wee was rounding third when Martin's catch killed the rally. Kuzava then put the Dodgers down without trouble in the eighth and ninth, and that was that.

Pee Wee batted a robust .345 for the series, his best ever, tying Duke Snider for the club leadership. He collected ten hits, scored three runs and batted in four.

During the series a rumor began floating about that Pee Wee had been offered the job of managing the Pirates. A reporter, checking on it, was told by Pee Wee, "Not me. First of all, nobody's even approached me for the job. Second of all, as I've said before, as long as I think I can play I don't want to manage." Then Pee Wee grinned, apparently in memory of his three hits the day before.

"And it looks like I may still have a couple of good years left."

CHAPTER **17**

It happened in Miami, that spring of 1953. The Dodgers,
finished with their day's workout, were dressing and drift-
ing in little groups back to their hotel. Pee Wee Reese,
usually one of the last to leave, was just getting out of the
shower. Jackie Robinson, though already dressed in his
street clothes, seemed to be deliberately lingering behind,
shuffling aimlessly through the equipment in his locker.

Finally, just the two men were left in the locker room.
Robinson walked down the file of lockers, making sure
all the players had gone. Then he closed the doors and
latched them. Pee Wee, toweling himself, just watched
Jackie quietly.

When he was satisfied that they were alone, Robinson
spoke up. "Pee Wee," he said, "something's come up that
I think you should know about. Or maybe you already
know about it—I don't know."

Reese nodded, "Go ahead, Jack."

"I thought we were through with this kind of thing
by now, but I guess we'll never see the end of it in our
lifetime. Crank letters, them I don't even think about
any more. But when the men on this team start talking
prejudice again, well, I just don't know what to do about
it. That's why I've come to you. I know where you stand."

"I've heard a few grumblings, seen a few funny looks," admitted Pee Wee. "You know what's causing it, Jackie?"

Robinson bit his lips. "Well, I'm supposed to be moving over to third, you know," he said, "because Junior Gilliam's going to be at second."

Robinson paused and Reese began to dress silently, waiting for him to go on.

"So the beef is this. When Joe Black's pitching, that means there'll be me, Gilliam, Black and Campanella on the field."

Pee Wee slipped on his trousers and began buttoning his shirt. "So what?" he said.

Robinson smiled, "I know that's what *you* think. But that's four Negro players, Pee Wee. Most of the fellows feel as you do. But there are a few who've been making remarks. You know the kind."

Pee Wee nodded. "You know who those players are?"

"Sure. But I don't want to name anybody. If you listen around you'll hear it soon enough. They're not trying to hide it."

"What do you think we should do about it, Jackie?"

"I don't know, really," Robinson said thoughtfully. "You know, Pee Wee, it's not a question of personal abuse any more. I've had worse than this. But if it continues, word'll get out to the papers and this thing might spread to some of the more suggestible fellows on the team. It could hurt our chances this year. It could ruin everything for us."

Reese made a neat knot in his tie, then slipped into a sports jacket. "Don't worry, Jackie. I'll do my best to straighten it out," he said.

"I know you will, Pee Wee. There's not a man on this team that doesn't have a world of respect for you."

As usual, Pee Wee's best was good enough. The few malcontents were straightened out, without any harshness or resulting friction, and the Dodgers came up to opening day ready to repeat the previous year's pennant victory.

A poll of the baseball writers made the Dodgers the favorites to win their second straight flag. The Phillies were second choice, the Giants third, the Cardinals fourth and the newly transplanted Milwaukee Braves fifth.

The Phillies jumped off to the lead, winning nine of their first eleven games. Then the Braves took over, and the surprising Milwaukee club held onto the lead through the first three weeks of June, while the Dodgers were either third or fourth, but never more than three games behind.

On June 26th, two games behind the Braves, the Dodgers arrived in Milwaukee for a three-game set. They won the first game, to cut the Braves' lead to one game. The second game was a tough one, with the Dodgers leading, 3–2, until their erstwhile teammate Andy Pafko tied the score with a homer in the ninth. That's the way it stood, 3–3, until the tenth inning.

Pee Wee Reese led off for the Dodgers in that inning. Jim Wilson, who had been pitching well for the Braves, got the usual first called strike on Pee Wee. Then he missed a curve for ball one. His next pitch was a fast ball, and Reese smashed it on a line into the left field bleachers for his sixth home run of the year.

That won it for Brooklyn, 4–3, and carried them into a tie with the Braves for first place. The following day the

Dodgers beat the Braves for the third straight time, taking over the league lead. They were never headed.

At the All-Star break, it was still a race. The Braves were a game and a half back of Brooklyn, while the Giants, in fifth place, were only six and a half games out. But as a kind of preview of what to expect afterward, Pee Wee Reese, for years the goat of the All-Star game, this time was the hero.

In his previous seven such contests, starting way back in 1942, Pee Wee didn't even have one hit to show for thirteen at bats. He missed out on his first two trips to the plate in this game, too. Then the goat started to shed his horns.

In the fifth inning, with the game scoreless, the National Leaguers went to work. With one out, Eddie Mathews was hit by a pitch. Enos Slaughter walked and Ashburn singled, scoring Mathews. Up came Pee Wee for his sixteenth try at an All-Star game hit. He swung at Reynolds' first pitch—maybe that was the answer—and singled to right, scoring Slaughter.

That wasn't all for Reese. In the seventh inning, with two out and Slaughter on base again, Pee Wee doubled to left center, for his second hit and run batted in. That made the score 3–0, in favor of the Nationals, who went on to win their fourth straight All-Star game, 5–1.

When regular play resumed, the Dodgers got hot, peeled off sixteen victories in nineteen games, breaking the race wide open. From the All-Star recess until September 1st, the Dodgers played at an incredible .820 pace. They won forty-one out of fifty during that stretch. On September 12th, Erskine beat the Braves, 5–2, to clinch the pennant.

The Dodgers had featured a murderous batting attack in running off with their second straight pennant. They hit two hundred and eight home runs, had a .285 team batting average. Even Pee Wee showed a little extra that year in the muscle department. He hit thirteen home runs and scored one hundred and eight times, while batting .271. And despite manager Dressen's comment the year before that Pee Wee was a poor sacrifice bunter, the Dodger captain led the league in sacrifice bunts, with fifteen.

In the base-stealing department, Pee Wee, who had led the league in 1952, came in second to Bill Bruton of Milwaukee, but he topped the Braves' center fielder in percentages of successful attempts. Reese stole twenty-two times in twenty-eight tries.

In this respect, Pee Wee stands as one of the best base stealers of all times. Aside from the fact that he is now the leading active National Leaguer in number of stolen bases, Pee Wee almost never gets caught in the attempt. Percentagewise, Reese's history shows that when he goes down for a steal, four out of five times he makes it.

This artistic thievery of Pee Wee's is one of Dodger coach Jake Pitler's favorite topics of discussion. "Reese is absolutely the smoothest guy taking a lead off first I ever saw," marvels Pitler. He gets as big a lead off as anyone in the business, and I remember seeing him picked off only twice.

"Pee Wee's secret is that he never gives away when he's ready to try to steal. He's quick. One second he's standing there, the next he's moving. That's all. No warning. It's all in his timing. He knows as much about every pitcher's moves as anybody, so he can get a good jump and be running in high before anybody even realizes he's going."

Pee Wee, however, along with the rest of the Dodgers, was still going nowhere as far as World Series competition was concerned. For all their pennant-winning power, the Dodgers went down to their fourth straight World Series loss to the Yankees, dropping the decision in six games. Pee Wee hit only .208 in this series. But at least—though it was doubtless of little satisfaction to Pee Wee—he committed none of the seven Dodger errors that materially hastened their downfall.

Two weeks after the series, it appeared that Pee Wee might finally become manager of the Dodgers. Charlie Dressen got into a disagreement with the front office that was impossible to disentangle. Walter O'Malley, the Dodgers' president, offered Dressen a one-year contract with a boost in salary. Dressen demanded a three-year contract. He felt that he was entitled to a longer contract since he had won several pennants for the Dodgers. Also since Durocher and other managers had been given longer contracts when the team hadn't done as well, he felt even more strongly. Neither side would come over to the other's way of thinking, so Dressen was soon without a job, Brooklyn without a manager.

The obvious choice to take Dressen's place at this point seemed to be Pee Wee, at least to many baseball observers. And despite the welter of confusion that surrounded the issue for the next few weeks, it was at least clear that O'Malley had considered Pee Wee the top candidate for the job.

What clouded the entire affair was the rather circumspect method the Dodgers brass used to sound out Pee Wee on his managerial intentions. Because while all reports had Pee Wee refusing the Dodgers' offer of the manager's post, it appeared at the same time that he'd never actually been offered it.

After Dressen was out, what happened was that Buzzy Bavasi, the vice-president, met Pee Wee in Columbus. "Did Bavasi offer you the manager's job then?" Pee Wee was asked.

Pee Wee could only smile. "Not exactly," he admitted. "Buzzy asked me that if such an offer were made to me would I accept it. I told him that for the present I wanted to continue as a player. We never got beyond that point in our discussion."

The conversation with Reese seemed to leave no doubt in Bavasi's mind and O'Malley's that Pee Wee did not want to manage the Dodgers. It was also obvious from their attitude that they did not want to exert any pressure on Pee Wee to take the job. As a matter of fact, had they exerted any pressure on Pee Wee, as little pressure as, for example, as simply telling him directly they'd like him to take it, Pee Wee would probably have been the next Dodger manager.

The Dodger front office must have known how little it would have taken to get Pee Wee to sign for the post. A week before Bavasi met with Pee Wee in Columbus, the Dodger captain had expressed his views on the matter, talking with sports writer Michael Gaven of the New York *Journal-American*.

"I can't say yes, I can't say no," said Pee Wee, when he was asked about his accepting the manager's job, "because no one connected with the Brooklyn club has asked me.

"There is only one thing I know for sure," Reese said. "That is I'm sorry Charlie quit. I called him and told him I hoped he'd change his mind. He's a good manager.

"It's never been my ambition to be an important person," Pee Wee continued. "I'm just a country boy who likes people and likes to talk to them, not duel with them. If anyone asked me two or three weeks ago if I would take the manager's job, the answer would have been definitely no. I figured that I have two or three years left in the majors and I want to run out my string in Brooklyn.

"I have never played major league baseball anywhere else, and my only minor league experience was right here in Louisville. So Brooklyn has always been home to me, and the Brooklyn club mighty good to me.

"Most ballplayers have played in a dozen or more minor and major league cities. But Dottie and I and our little girl have been very lucky in that respect. We have lived only in Louisville, our home town, and Brooklyn.

"So now," Pee Wee went on, "if Mr. O'Malley or Buzzy Bavasi should come to me and tell me that because this thing happened so suddenly they had no one else ready for the job, I could hardly say no simply because it would give me more work. Of course I couldn't. I owe them enough allegiance and loyalty at least to listen to their proposition. . . ."

So Bavasi must have known this was how Pee Wee felt when he went to Columbus later to talk to him. But all he asked Reese was whether Pee Wee would accept such an offer were it made to him. Whether this was the Dodgers' method of avoiding direct pressure on Reese and allowing him to refuse gracefully, or whether there were other reasons for the vague offer to Pee Wee, remains a moot question.

The only thing that could be said for certain was that the end result found Walter Alston managing the Dodgers in 1954.

CHAPTER 18

The terrible joke about Walter Alston was that the
Dodgers hired him to beat the Yankees in the World
Series, and he didn't even win the pennant. Poor Alston,
however, had the same bad luck his predecessor Charlie
Dressen had, that of taking over the Dodgers in one of
their jinx years. With Dressen, it was Thomson's home
run in the '51 play-offs. With Alston, the first-year hoodoo
didn't wait that long. As soon as they realized that catcher
Roy Campanella's injured hand would cripple him for
the season, baseball men shook their heads. Without Roy's
powerful bat, the Dodgers would be in sad shape.

All things considered, even some of Alston's early sec-
ond-guessers had to concede the Dodgers did well to stay
in the race as long as they did. Aside from Campanella's
injury, Reese missed nine important games with a leg
injury, and at various times nearly every member of the
pitching staff complained of a sore arm.

Only Carl Erskine showed any kind of hurling effec-
tiveness, but even he lost almost as often as he won. Don
Newcombe, who was expected to be the big man of the
staff, was a bust, winning only nine games.

Still, the Dodgers hung on the Giants' trail until the
bitter end. With Reese, Robinson and Snider leading the

hitting attack and Erskine providing most of the pitching, they managed to make things interesting.

Pee Wee, particularly, was having a great year at the plate. In one night game in June, he practically mopped up Ebbets Field with the Braves as the Dodgers won, 8–4. He hit a home run and a double, scored two runs and batted in four, besides starting two double plays. The homer, his eighth of the year, was also Pee Wee's one hundredth of his career.

A couple of weeks later, running out a triple against the Giants, Pee Wee slid into third and wrenched a muscle in his thigh. Some of the pessimistic oracles in baseball circles took this as a sign of Pee Wee's advancing years.

"Reese'll never get back into shape," they prophesied, shaking their heads sadly. "When a ballplayer gets to be thirty-five, like Reese, the muscles don't respond like they used to. The Dodgers are really finished now."

Well, they were half right, anyhow. The Dodgers, it turned out, weren't going anywhere but second place. But Pee Wee bounced back from his injury like a kid out of high school.

He broke into the line-up again on July 8th, after missing nine games. In his first four games he got nine hits, including two doubles and a triple, and drew four walks. And he kept going. In Cincinnati, he broke up a tie game with his ninth homer of the year. A week later his tenth home run and a single won another ball game. For a twenty-three-game stretch after injuring his foot, Pee Wee hit at better than a .400 clip, raising his season's average to .311.

On Reese's thirty-fifth birthday, July 23rd, the Dodgers

lost to the Cardinals. Up in the press box during the game sat Eddie Stanky, the Red Bird manager, waiting out a five-day suspension. In the ninth inning there were two out for Brooklyn and a runner on second when Junior Gilliam came to bat against Vic Raschi.

"Come on, Vic Damone!" yelled Stanky, using his pet name for Raschi. "Get this guy out, I don't want 'Happy Birthday' to get up there."

Stanky, paying tribute to Pee Wee's reputation as a clutch hitter, knew a situation like this would be just the spot for Reese to get a hit that would beat the Cardinals. Eddie breathed a sign of relief when Gilliam popped out to end the game, denying Reese the opportunity.

As the Dodgers' chances faded, even the veteran players became despondent. But Pee Wee refused to give up, at least outwardly.

"You've got to watch yourself," he told a sports writer, explaining part of the strain that comes with being team captain. "You've got to have false pepper. You have to say things to guys. You have to keep telling yourself things, too."

Later, Pitcher Russ Meyer explained how Pee Wee helped him over the rough spots. "You get a little wild," Meyer said. "You walk a guy and you get behind on the next guy. You figure you don't have your stuff and you lose your confidence. Then Pee Wee comes over and says you're okay, your stuff's good. And when Pee Wee tells you that, you believe him."

Junior Gilliam, standing next to Meyer, added to the pitcher's praise of Reese. "He keeps my spirits up," said Gilliam. "I let a ball go by and he tells me things that make me feel good when I'm down in the dumps."

But there was no escaping the inevitable that year. The Giants, who seemed to do everything right just when the Dodgers were slumping, eased into the pennant.

Pee Wee, for once, conquered his old habit of tailing off in his hitting toward the close of a campaign. From mid-July until the final day, he led all Dodger hitters with .322. In September he hit .352 and wound up the year with the best hitting average of his career—.309, twenty-three points better than his previous high set in 1951.

But Pee Wee's pleasure was tempered. "I'd give it back and take a .260," said Pee Wee, "if it would mean we'd have won the pennant."

Coming from Pee Wee, there was no doubting the sincerity of feeling—which is one reason why, perhaps, that in a poll taken during the season's final week, Pee Wee Reese was acclaimed the all-time favorite of Dodger fans. And why, too, during the height of the Dodgers' successful 1955 season, on the eve of his birthday, "Pee Wee Reese Night" was one of the most sincere and successful affairs of its kind.

As Jimmy Cannon, sports columnist for the New York *Post,* commented, "I generally ignore such nights because the promotion department plots them. . . . But every game Brooklyn plays is a sort of Reese night. Ask the players. They know him better than I do. . . .

"Fortunate is the guy who has Reese for a friend," Cannon said. And there isn't anyone on the Dodgers who isn't close to him in some way. There have been better ballplayers, but I've never heard anyone who claimed there was a finer guy. It's too bad the guides don't print such information. It tells more than batting averages."

There was Walter Alston, too, talking about Pee Wee before the game that marked "Pee Wee Reese Night."

"What makes Pee Wee Reese tick?" Alston repeated a writer's question. He thought for a minute, then replied, "Character, natural ability, versatility, intelligence and a habit of placing his team ahead of Harold Reese at all times."

To Roy Campanella, lacing on his spikes in the locker room before the game, it went deeper than that.

"It's great to see a night like this for a fellow who deserves it as much as Reese. All round the league, everybody knows he's never been bad. That's a lot to say about a man.

"But I know there's even more in my own heart. When we first came up here he was the guy who went out of the way for us. That doesn't have to be publicized or known in the street, but I know it down deep."

As for Pee Wee himself, embarrassed and a little scared and wishing he didn't have to go out into the spotlight on the field, he had just one thing to say.

"I just hope we win the game," he said. "I can stand most anything if we win."

The Dodgers did win it, making it a perfect "happy birthday" for Pee Wee, and his own contribution to the 8–4 festivities with the Braves was a pair of doubles, each resulting in a run.

The 1955 pennant, of course, was a cakewalk for the Dodgers. After they set a record by winning their first ten games of the season, the rest was easy. Even though they actually played only fair ball during the latter half of the summer, the rest of the contenders could do no better, and the pennant was clinched early in September.

The only sour note in the entire proceedings was that Pee Wee, for the first time since 1941, was not named to the All-Star team. Ernie Banks, the young Chicago Cub shortstop, was selected in the voting, and All-Star manager Leo Durocher chose the Milwaukee Braves' Johnny Logan as the number two man.

There was some feeling among the New York sports writers that Durocher had chosen Logan, because the game was to be played in Milwaukee. And Jackie Robinson, always ready to speak on behalf of Reese, criticized both selections. "I'll take Pee Wee over the two shortstops named."

Reese, however, refused to agree with Robinson. "I'll miss playing in the All-Star game," he admitted. "And I mean that sincerely. But the fans picked Ernie Banks and I think Durocher took the right man in Johnny Logan."

This was one time the sports writing fraternity did not support the Dodger captain's opinion.

The second time came before the World Series. Pee Wee predicted that this time the Dodgers would beat the Yankees, a feeling not shared by the majority of baseball observers. The Dodgers may have looked better on paper, but there seemed to be some psychological block that made them play like patsies against the Yankees.

But Reese didn't hold with that analysis. "If our pitching comes through, we'll win, no matter who we play," said Pee Wee. "Besides," he added with a grin. "I'm the only guy in history who ever played in five World Series without winning one—and always against the same team. How long can it last?"

As it turned out, it lasted only another seven days.

CHAPTER 19

The Dodgers were really confident of beating the Yankees this time. They had pitching, they had power, they had depth. And when they jumped on Yankee ace Whitey Ford for two runs in the second inning of the World Series opener, they figured they were on their way.

Furillo started it with a homer. Robinson tripled, Zimmer singled and it was quickly 2–0 Brooklyn. But Don Newcombe, the Dodgers twenty-game winner, couldn't stand the prosperity. In the Yankee half of the second, Collins walked and Elston Howard homered to tie the score. Snider homered for Brooklyn in the third, but the Yankees tied it again in their half. Collins' homer in the fourth put the Yanks in front and his second homer with one on in the sixth made it 6–3 Yankees. The Dodgers' two-run rally in the eighth was not enough.

After the Yankees' great comeback pitcher Tommy Byrne beat the Dodgers, 4–2, in the second game, only the most stouthearted of Dodger supporters would have given a nickel for their chances of winning the series.

Numbered among the stouthearted Dodger supporters, of course, was Pee Wee Reese.

In the Dodger dressing room before the third game, the Dodger captain spoke quietly and informally to his teammates. "Okay," he said. "So now we're two games down. That'll make the victory taste even better. Remember, guys, during the season when they had us shut out, even no-hitted for six and seven innings, and we came back to win it?

"Well, there's no reason why we can't do the same thing now. The Yankees aren't any better than the Braves—or the Giants or the Cardinals. And remember this, fellas, before this series started everybody was saying we choke up when we play the Yankees. If we lose to them again . . . well, maybe we'll just have to admit we've got no guts."

The Dodgers took the field that day a grim bunch of ballplayers. And the Yankee pitcher Bob Turley felt the difference in them fast.

He disposed of Gilliam to open the contest, but Reese waited the erratic fireballer out and drew a pass. Snider was an out, but Roy Campanella cracked a home run into the left field stands for a 2-0 yead. As in the first two games in Yankee Stadium, the Bronx Bombers struck right back with two runs in the second. But this time the ending was to be different.

With one out, the Dodgers loaded the bases in their half of the second on a single, a walk and a hit batsman. When Turley walked Gilliam, forcing in a run, Tom Morgan came in to relieve. Again Pee Wee worked himself a pass, forcing in the second run. The Dodgers added two more in the fourth and two more in the sixth, Pee Wee driving in the final run with a single. It was an 8-3 victory for young Johnny Podres, who was destined to make history for the Dodgers in a few more days.

The Dodger big guns continued their barrage in the fourth game. The Yankees got off to a 3-1 lead, after three and a half frames, but the Dodgers, under the calm urging of manager Alston and captain Reese, weren't fooling around any more. In the bottom half of the fourth Campanella homered, Furillo singled and Hodges homered. Just like that it was 4–3 Brooklyn.

In the fifth the Dodgers applied the crusher to the game. Gilliam opened with a walk. Don Larsen went two balls and no strikes to Reese, then was lifted for Johnny Kucks. Pee Wee greeted the reliever with a wicked smash between first and second. Joe Collins made a great stab of the ball, but Kucks couldn't cover first in time and it went for a hit. Snider then broke it up with the Dodgers third homer of the day. Final score, 8–5, and the series was tied at two games apiece.

Riding the crest of the wave now, the Dodgers made their first bit of history by beating the Yankees for the third straight time, 5–3, marking the first time in a World Series a team lost the first two games and came back to win the next three. But all kinds of records were to fall by the wayside before this series was in the books.

The series reverted to Yankee Stadium for the sixth game, and the old pro Yankees evened the score by beating Brooklyn, 5–1, on a beautiful four-hitter by Whitey Ford. The Dodgers' only run came in the fourth when Reese singled, Campanella walked and Furillo singled Pee Wee home.

So the stage was now set for the dramatic seventh game.

It was just a little past noon. The Dodger clubhouse was deserted except for Roy Campanella, Pee Wee Reese and pitcher Johnny Podres.

"Just get that change-up over like you did the other

day," Campanella said to Podres, who had beaten the Yankees in the third series game.

Pee Wee nodded. "Pitch 'em the way Campy calls 'em, Johnny, and we'll make it. Remember, you don't have to strike 'em all out. We're behind you. Just take it easy. Take your time and pitch to your spots. This is just another ball game."

The young left-hander was pale, but he smiled. "Don't worry. I'll get the ball over. Get me some runs and we'll win."

Then the three men walked out of the clubhouse to face the Yankees in the final game of the 1955 World Series, the roly-poly, good-humored catcher, veteran of the tough grind of the Negro leagues, the twenty-three-year-old pitcher, with the load of the world on his young shoulders, and the thirty-six-year-old shortstop who had turned down a manager's job so he could continue to play ball.

For two innings Podres and Tommy Byrne maintained a scoreless deadlock. Byrne got the Dodgers out in the third. In the Yankee third, Podres got the first two. But Rizzuto walked and Billy Martin singled to right, sending the Scooter to second. Then Podres got behind Mc-Dougald, three balls and one strike. Pee Wee Reese called time.

The Dodger captain walked to the mound, where he was joined by Campanella. "Got your control, Johnny?" Reese asked calmly.

Podres nodded, "I'm okay."

"Just keep the pitch down, Johnny," Pee Wee said. "And take your time."

Campanella punched the pocket of his mitt. "Put it on his fists, Johnny, we'll get him."

The two men went back to their positions and Podres stood alone on the mound. He reached down, picked up the rosin bag, squeezed it a couple of times and dropped it. Then he wound up and pitched to McDougald.

The Yankee infielder swung and hit a low bouncer down the third base line. It was a tough play for third baseman Hoak, but the Dodgers got a break when the ball hit Rizzuto as he slid into the bag for an automatic out that closed the inning.

Back on the bench, Podres let out his breath. "That was a close one," he said.

Reese smiled. "Those are the kind you need. This looks like your day, Johnny. Just play it cool."

In the fourth inning the Dodgers got their first hit off Byrne—and their first run. With one out, Campanella doubled, went to third on Furillo's infield out and scored on Hodges' single to left. But that one run didn't look too big, what with all the home run hitting that had gone before.

In the Yankees' fourth, Berra lifted a fly to left center. It was an easy chance, but Snider and Gilliam got their signals crossed and the ball dropped in for a double. Podres kicked at the dirt with his toe.

"That's as far as he goes, Johnny," Reese called. "Nobody else gets lucky this inning."

Podres bore down and got Bauer on a fly to right. Moose Skowron stepped in to hit and Campanella trotted out to the mound.

"Shake me off once," the catcher said. "Get him guessing what we're goin' to throw."

Skowron grounded to Zimmer at second, and Podres got Bob Cerv on a pop to Reese.

The Dodgers scored their second run off Byrne in the fifth. Pee Wee started it off with a single. Snider was safe on an error. Campanella sacrificed and Furillo was passed intentionally. With the bases loaded, Hodges lifted a fly to deep center and Reese crossed the plate to make the score 2–0. Hoak walked, but Shuba, batting for Zimmer, grounded out.

As things turned out, that unsuccessful pinch hit may have saved the day for Brooklyn. For with Zimmer out, Gilliam was shifted to second base, while Amoros took over in left field, which meant that minutes later Sandy was there to make a vital catch that the less-experienced Gilliam probably wouldn't have made.

Martin opened the Yankees' sixth by drawing a walk, and McDougald dropped a perfect bunt for a hit. That put the tying runs on and nobody out. Yogi Berra stepped in and Reese called time.

Manager Alston joined the group at the mound now. "You all right, Johnny?" Alston asked.

Podres nodded.

"He got out of it with two on before," Reese put in. "He can do it again."

"Take it easy now," Campanella said. "Nothing too good to this guy. We can't let him pull." Then he turned to Alston. "He'll be okay."

Podres got Berra to hit an outside pitch, but the ball sliced down the left field foul line. With Amoros swung around to right on the left-hand batter, it looked like a sure hit. But the fleet-footed Amoros never gave up on it. "Get it, Sandy, get it," Podres prayed, as Amoros raced at top speed across the outfield, stuck out his glove at the last moment—and caught the ball!

The fielder skidded to a stop just before the stands, whirled and threw into the infield. The throw was high. Reese, who went up in the air for the ball, saw that Mc-Dougald had come too far off first base. As he came down with the ball, Pee Wee turned and fired in one motion to Hodges, doubling off McDougald.

It was a beautiful exhibition of defensive skill, and the double play broke the Yankees' back.

In the eighth inning the Bombers made their last desperate bid. Rizzuto, fighting heroically to the very end, opened with a single to left. Martin flied out. The pesky McDougald smashed a wicked hopper to third that bounced off Hoak's shoulder for a single. Rizzuto wound up on third.

Again Pee Wee walked to the mound. "You're doing great," Reese said. "Just remember, if the ball's hit to you, come to me with it."

Podres looked at Berra, who was standing off to the side of the batter's box. "What's the price he's going to try to hit it out of here," he said matter-of-factly.

"Let him try," Reese grinned.

Campanella trotted up. "If we get behind on this guy, give him your fast ball. Don't hold anything back—but not inside to him."

Podres nodded. He got behind on Berra, three and one. Then he came in with his fast ball. Berra lifted an easy fly to Furillo. Campanella signaled for the fast one again and Podres fanned Bauer. The crowd thundered its cheers.

Podres made short work of the Yankees in the ninth.

Skowron went out. Cerv went out. After Podres slipped a quick strike past Elston Howard, Reese ran over from short.

"Easy, Johnny. Don't try too hard. Just put it in there. We'll get him out." Pee Wee trotted back to his position.

Podres looked down for the sign from Campanella. He went to two-and-two on Howard. He shook off Campanella's sign. He shook it off again. Then he pitched.

It was a very appropriate ending. Howard grounded to Pee Wee Reese. Pee Wee swallowed the ball with his glove, picked it out, threw it to Hodges—and the World Series was over.

Who could accurately describe what happened after that? The Dodgers were World Champions, something no other Dodger team in history had been able to declare, and Brooklyn and Brooklyn fans everywhere let out all the stops in celebration.

The Dodgers mobbed Podres and the crowd at Yankee Stadium broke through the special police cordon to add their congratulations to the young left-hander who had pitched so brilliantly.

Outside the environs of the ball field, pandemonium broke loose. Caravans of automobiles roamed the streets of Brooklyn all the rest of the afternoon and night, tooting horns and blowing whistles. People marched the streets, banging on pots and pans, business came to a halt, showers of confetti and shredded paper streamed down from office windows. Bosses shook hands with their employees, and a neighborhood delicatessen handed out free hot dogs to everybody.

At the Dodgers' victory dinner, Pee Wee's mother, who had come from Louisville to see the series, spoke quietly.

"I prayed for Pee Wee right along to be in a winning World Series against the Yankees," she said.

"He had waited so long. He played in five series against the Yankees and every time the Dodgers were beaten. So now I'm happy. He finally did it and it doesn't matter much what happens now.

"Of course," she added, "I only hope he keeps on playing, and I'm sure he will. But this was the big thing, being on a winning World Series team just once."

CHAPTER 20

The familiar noises of men at play came to them as they stood there on the baseball field, the veteran sports reporter and the newcomer on his first visit to a spring training camp. There was the hard, clean sound of horsehide meeting wood, the shrill cries of the fielders, the patient voices of the coaches directing the practice session.

"So this is Vero Beach, winter home of the World Champion Brooklyn Dodgers," said the younger man.

"This is it," agreed the veteran, sniffing the air contentedly, like an old hound dog recognizing the scent of a familiar scent .

"Most of the regulars aren't down here yet. These kids are tryouts, the ones on the field now. Up from the minors, maybe, for a look. Or maybe just sandlotters trying to break in."

"It must be funny," said the other. "I mean, after you've been covering baseball ten or fifteen years. You're writing about the top guys, famous players, and you remember when they were nothing, like these kids here."

"It's true," agreed the veteran. "I've seen them all come up. Take the Dodger line-up from top to bottom, I remember them all. And I've seen them come and go."

"It must be a great feeling," said the younger man.

The other shook his head. "No. It just makes me feel old."

A ball broke loose from the playing field and bounced over to where the two men were standing. The older man stooped over and picked up the ball, then threw it with an awkward motion back to the diamond.

"The oldest guy on the Dodgers now is Reese," the veteran continued. "And I can picture him like it was yesterday, a pale, scared-looking kid up from Louisville. He was supposed to take away Leo Durocher's job, and he looked more like a bat boy than a baseball player.

"And that, my young friend, was sixteen years ago."

"There's one thing I've always wondered about Pee Wee," the other said. "He's been such a great player with the Dodgers for so long, how come he's never won a Most Valuable Player award?"

The veteran writer thought a minute. "That's a good question. And it has a lot of answers. Maybe the best one is that the MVP always goes to the guy with the impressive statistics. A pitcher with a lot of wins, a batter with a high average or a lot of home runs or runs batted in. But you can't measure the greatness of Reese with a slide rule. He's a great performer, sure. But it's more than that, something emotional, human. It's something about the way he makes playing with the Dodgers a happy experience, about the way he is with new men, and with the veterans, too, making them work together smoothly.

"I think it was Hal Schumacher of the Giants who once said, 'Take Pee Wee Reese and any eight men and you've got a team.' No, you won't find the greatness of Pee Wee in the record books."

"And yet," said the young reporter, "he has the reputation of being one of the toughest clutch hitters in the game."

"That's a fact," acknowledged the other. "You ask the best pitchers in the league, they'll tell you that when the chips are down, when that one little hit is needed to tie or win a ball game, the two Dodgers they fear the most are Reese and Jackie Robinson. And Jackie usually bats a good twenty or thirty points higher than Pee Wee.

"And another thing. Reese, if you've been watching him down through the years, is the kind of player that starts off a rally. When you're having trouble with a pitcher, Pee Wee'll get that walk or that single that starts things off."

"Well," said the younger man, "I wonder what's goin' to be the story with him this year? The Dodgers can't sit on Zimmer and Fernandez forever. They're too good."

"Maybe so," said the other. "Then again, I've seen shortstops come up before who were going to make Pee Wee move over. I think the first one, right after the war, was Stan Rojek. Then, let's see . . . there were Bob Ramazzotti, Gene Mauch, Bobby Morgan, Eddie Miksis, Rocky Bridges, then Zimmer for the past couple of years —and now Fernandez.

"Maybe this year it'll happen, then again maybe it won't. For all we know, the guy who's destined to make Pee Wee move over may be out there now," the veteran said, indicating the youngsters on the playing field. "Some guy we never even heard of yet."

"You know," the young sports writer said, "we may be talking for nothing. The Dodgers have already talked with Pee Wee and decided what's what for the year."

"It wouldn't surprise me," admitted the veteran. "Though I'd probably have heard something about it by now. Anyway, we'll soon find out. Unless my eyes are even worse than I think, that's Pee Wee coming over this way now."

The two men watched silently as the good-looking man in slacks and open-collared sports shirt approached them from the far end of the field. He walked along the foul line, stopping here and there where a man was fungo hitting to shake a familiar hand and exchange a few words of greeting.

"Hi, Pee Wee," the veteran greeted the man when he came up to them.

Reese's face broke into a dimpled grin and he put out his hand. "Hey, haven't they retired you to the boneyard yet?" he said.

The old sports writer grinned back. "I'm not going till you go," he returned, gripping Reese's hand warmly. Then the two old friends talked about what they had done over the winter, bringing each other up to date on what was new around the baseball beat. Finally, the sports writer said to Pee Wee, "Well, how about it, Pee Wee, where are you playing this year? Shortstop again? Or have they got you moving to third or second or someplace?"

Reese looked surprised for a moment. "To tell the truth, I don't know. I hope I'll be playing shortstop, naturally. But if it'll help the team and keep me in Brooklyn, I'll play whatever they ask me to."

"You haven't discussed this with Alston yet?"

"No, and now that you mention it, I think it would be a good idea if I did check with Walt to see what the score is. You see him around here anyplace?"

The sports writer pointed toward a dugout. He was down in his office last I saw of him," he said. "Good luck," he added as Reese started away.

Pee Wee stopped for a moment and looked back. "Yeah, thanks." he smiled, then he went down the dugout steps and disappeared under the stands.

Reese walked into the managerial sanctum of Walter "Smokey" Alston's, for the first time not quite sure of himself. The curtain has to ring down for everybody someday, he thought philosophically. He stopped before the Dodger manager's desk and took a deep breath. "Skip," he said, "where am I playing this year?"

Alston looked up at Reese, a funny half-smile on his face.

"Shortstop. Where else?"

Reese simply nodded and strode from the room. He went into the Dodger clubhouse, opened his locker, stripped off his street clothes and changed hurriedly into the buff and blue Dodger uniform with the big No. 1 on its back. Then he slammed the locker door shut and walked out of the clubhouse.

The long hallway leading to the playing field was dark and cool, and Pee Wee walked its length slowly, working his fingers into the infielder's glove on his left hand, listening to the clatter of his spiked shoes on the concrete walk.

As he neared the yellow oblong of light at the end of the corridor his steps quickened, until at last he burst into the hot brightness of the Florida afternoon. He bounded up the steps of the dugout, eyes sparkling, and walked swiftly across the emerald greenness of the infield to his position at shortstop.

INDEX